Ready, BEGIN!

Practical Strategies
for
Cultivating Courage

Lawrence M. Kryske

Trafford Publishing
Canada ◆ USA ◆ UK ◆ Europe

This book is intended to provide information concerning the subject matter covered. It is sold with the understanding that the author is not engaged in rendering legal, medical, psychological, or other professional services other than those which he is qualified to provide. If legal, medical, psychological, or other expert assistance is required, the services of competent professionals should be sought.

This book is not an attempt to be an exhaustive reference for all the subjects that lie between these covers. You are urged to read all available information on these subjects to give you the broadest and most complete discussion possible. Every effort has been made to make this book as accurate as possible. There may, however, be mistakes, both of a typographical nature and involving content. Accordingly, use this book with the proviso that it is a general guide and not the ultimate source of information on these subjects.

Since the purpose of this book is to educate, the author has no liability or responsibility to any person or entity with respect to any loss or damage caused, or alleged to be caused, directly or indirectly by the information contained in this book.

Cover design by: Debbie Romero

Order this book online at www.trafford.com/07-2988
or email orders@trafford.com

Most Trafford titles are also available at major online book retailers.

Note for Librarians: A cataloguing record for this book is available from Library and Archives Canada at www.collectionscanada.ca/amicus/index-e.html

ISBN: 978-1-4251-6478-2

We at Trafford believe that it is the responsibility of us all, as both individuals and corporations, to make choices that are environmentally and socially sound. You, in turn, are supporting this responsible conduct each time you purchase a Trafford book, or make use of our publishing services. To find out how you are helping, please visit www.trafford.com/responsiblepublishing.html

Our mission is to efficiently provide the world's finest, most comprehensive book publishing service, enabling every author to experience success. To find out how to publish your book, your way, and have it available worldwide, visit us online at www.trafford.com/10510

Trafford PUBLISHING   www.trafford.com

North America & international
toll-free: 1 888 232 4444 (USA & Canada)
phone: 250 383 6864 ♦ fax: 250 383 6804 ♦ email: info@trafford.com

The United Kingdom & Europe
phone: +44 (0)1865 722 113 ♦ local rate: 0845 230 9601
facsimile: +44 (0)1865 722 868 ♦ email: info.uk@trafford.com

10 9 8 7 6 5 4 3 2 1

Acknowledgements

During my twenty-two years in the U.S. Navy, I witnessed firsthand many heroic deeds and personal sacrifices. This book, in part, draws from the memory of those acts of courage.

I sincerely appreciate the assistance from Patrick H. Booth, Harry Cash, Royce Cumbest, Paul Gottlieb, Dr. Stephen Gruber, Captain H. Wyman Howard, G. Dulany Howland, Jerry Johnsen, Rear Admiral Curt Kemp, Richard H. Knight, Jr., Kyle Kryske, Leon E. Kryske, Paul Kryske, Richard Langworth, Charles V. Lemmon, Dr. Hylan B. Lyon, Jr., Ryan Malphurs, and especially my wife, Naomi. Thank you all! Joshua 1:9.

Dedication

To Master Chief Jay Piper, a retired U.S. Navy bandmaster who donated his entire collection of Churchill books to me (via the Churchill Centre) after Hurricane Katrina claimed mine. Among his books was Princess Bibesco's *Sir Winston Churchill: Master of Courage.* That book started me thinking about developing a practical book about courage. Thank you, Jay, for throwing me a line!

Table of Contents

civic groups, education, or at home. Strong courageous leadership is needed everywhere.

This book answers the mail where other leadership books have been vague or silent about how to be courageous. I have derived my insights and suggestions from over forty years of leadership study and scholarship, over thirty years leading teams as well as serving on scores of them, twenty-two years of wearing the uniform of my country, and twelve years guiding hundreds of diverse organizations to be better at leadership.

To quote Vietnam POW Charlie Plumb, "I'm no hero." But I did know some heroic people, I have witnessed some heroic deeds, and I am aware of a great deal of heroic behavior.

Larry Kryske
January 24, 2008

Introduction

What separates the almost great from the great? What transforms a leader into a legend? What enables a business to adopt new changes successfully or embrace quality? What permits a sales person to leave the pack behind? What allows a person to do what is right despite enduring public ridicule and personal loss? The answer is COURAGE!

Courage is critical to a multitude of facets involving leadership and business success:

- Conquering procrastination
- Creating bolder visions
- Overcoming fear and anxiety
- Inspiring commitment
- Empowering action
- Excelling at sales
- Encouraging innovation
- Integrating quality

- Exceeding customer expectations
- Facilitating change
- Embracing integrity and accountability
- Strengthening team cohesiveness
- Sustaining momentum

Leadership is the art of getting things done with other people. The most important words in this definition are "getting things done." Leadership is not solely about planning, intentions, dreaming, or hopes. Rather it involves achieving specific, measurable, time-dependent outcomes. Visioning and planning are only part of the leadership equation. Translating those visions into reality takes courage and determination.

> **"Be courageous! I have seen many depressions in business. Always America has come out stronger and more prosperous. Be as brave as your fathers before you. Have faith! Go forward."**
> **Thomas A. Edison**

In every business endeavor courage is necessary to be successful. In sales courage is needed to overcome the fear of making cold calls, of failure and rejection, of making a sales presentation, and of asking for the sale. In change management courage is needed to create a compelling vision, to communicate honestly with all employees, to give ownership to stakeholders, to build momentum, and to cut through bureaucracy and naysayers to achieve short-term wins.

Being innovative means courageously offending sacred cows and conventional wisdom, creating a playful environment that stimulates new ideas, and doing things in a totally different way. Implementing quality improvement takes courage. It also takes courage to reconsider processes before blindly assuming that people problems are to blame.

Executives, managers, and supervisors need to be with their people, leading them, not behind their desks. That takes courage. They confront doubts, cynicism, and ridicule to get the mission done. That takes courage. Where physical danger, adversity, and hardship are present, so are leaders. That takes courage. Balanced risks, bold visions, and dramatic acts become the rule not the exception. That takes courage!

I've been amazed by the volume and variety of leadership books currently in print. Many of these books cite historical figures who had courage and explain why courage is a critical leadership trait. Unfortunately, the authors fail to tell the reader exactly how to be courageous. There are, however, a number of things a person can do to prepare his or her body, mind, and spirit to be courageous when the occasion arises.

No one ever graduates from the school of leadership or courage. We are all students. Whenever someone thinks that he or she has arrived, a more complex, challenging opportunity presents itself.

****

A man stood facing a blank canvas. His vision was to capture in oils the peaceful countryside before him. He was a great leader—he eventually walked the world's stage for over seventy years, served in five wars, and authored over fifty books—but this leader didn't feel great in front of the canvas. He was intimidated by the empty white surface that stared back at him. Brush in hand, he hesitated. Then he timidly put a tiny dab of blue paint on the canvas—blue since the sky was blue. And this great leader was anxious about what to do next.

Don't we all have a blank canvas before us? Aren't we waiting to paint our masterpiece on it? However, instead of oils, we paint by what we say and do. So what's keeping us from reaching our dreams?

And what's holding our organizations back? We've set goals. We've developed mission statements, vision statements, and value statements. And we've identified strategic objectives. Despite having a crystal-clear picture of where we want to go, the outcomes we desire continue to elude us.

Keeping pace in today's global market means changing the way we do business. Unfortunately, we tend to regard change with the same enthusiasm as volunteering for a root canal. Implementing change takes bold leadership.

Most people remember Winston Churchill for his dynamic presence as the Prime Minister of Great Britain during the Second World War. He perceived the coming of both world wars and the Cold War. He had a bulldog's courage and a never-give-in attitude. And he used heroic words and deeds to change the way people thought.

Churchill was one of the truly great Renaissance men of all time. He was a statesman and warrior, an administrator and historian, an orator and bricklayer. He was also an accomplished artist. He managed to complete over six hundred oil paintings sandwiched between his other career achievements. Yet he was the great leader intimidated by that blank canvas. His painting career almost ended before it began.

How did Churchill overcome his hesitation at the canvas? He needed the help of a friend to show him the way. In a similar fashion, this book will serve as your guide. I'll share with you some insights and suggestions on how we can make our visions a reality. To do this, we need to expand our visioning process, because vision alone isn't enough.

Churchill was once called a young man in a hurry. His productivity and achievements were prodigious. His leadership and life are best described by a three-step strategy for success.

First, he needed a compelling vision of what he wanted to achieve. Then he needed the courage to take those critical first steps. And finally, he needed to follow through with determination until he achieved his vision. Vision, courage, determination—I call these key factors the Churchill Factors. (Appendix A gives a more detailed summary of the Churchill Factors.)

> **"Courage is rightly esteemed the first of human qualities because it is the quality which guarantees all others."**
> **Winston S. Churchill**

Most people can craft a vision. And, if they can just get started, they can perhaps plod along until they achieve their goals. But taking those first steps often becomes a barrier to them. They need courage to move beyond their vision.

Although we can cultivate the soil, put a seed in the ground, water and fertilize it, we cannot make the fruit develop on an accelerated time schedule. Bearing fruit will only happen if the conditions are right for the plant.

Cultivation merely involves loosening up the soil to foster the future growth of the plant. In a similar fashion, cultivating courage means identifying the nature of courage and discovering ways to develop the thinking, reflexes, and actions that will help a person become courageous.

The Five Cornerstones of Courage™ will provide a means to understand the nature of courage and offer a variety of practical ways to cultivate it. Courage is the objective we pursue. Whether we attain this purpose will ultimately be up to each individual.

Summary of Key Points

- Leaders respond to life's challenges with vision, courage, and determination.
- Courage is the most important leadership trait.
- A person sources courage from the inside out.

1

The Nature of Courage

Courage has many names:

- Boldness
- Valor
- Heroism
- Daring
- Intrepidness
- Bravery
- Pluck

- Audacity
- Fearlessness
- Gallantry
- True grit
- Sand
- Mettle
- Fortitude

Courage also has been referred to as having:

- Guts
- Cheek
- Backbone
- Nerve

- Heart
- Face
- And some other anatomical parts!

Things courage makes possible:

- Leading a team to victory
- Public speaking
- Devotion to duty
- Standing up for the underdog
- Asking for that first date
- Serving as a missionary
- Asking for the sale
- Preventing an airliner from being used as a missile to attack the White House
- Telling the boss what he needs to hear, not what he necessarily wants to hear
- Refusing to sacrifice standards of safety
- Going where no one has gone before
- Forming up at the scrimmage line against a bigger, stronger team
- Taking an unpopular stand
- Protecting the innocent from harm and evil
- Asking for a pay raise
- Tough love
- Signing the Declaration of Independence
- Buying that first home
- Answering a cry for help
- Serving in the military or as a police officer, firefighter, paramedic, first responder
- Looking for a solution to a difficult problem

When we consider this list, we can understand why Sir James Barrie, creator of *Peter Pan* said, "Courage is the thing. All goes if courage goes."

Wikipedia, the internet encyclopedia, has defined courage as, "the ability to confront fear, pain, risk, danger, uncertainty or intimidation. 'Physical courage' is courage in the face of physical pain, hardship, or threat of death. 'Moral courage' is the courage to act rightly in the face of popular opposition, shame, scandal, or discouragement." These are appropriate definitions of courage.

We can have courage by the color—the red badge of courage and the Purple Heart. A number of animals symbolize courage in different cultures: the lion, eagle, tiger, and bear. A person might resort to Dutch or liquid courage like the British soldiers who were given a rum ration before going over the top during World War I.

Courage occupies a prominent position as one of four classical Western virtues, along with wisdom, moderation, and justice. Dr. Stephen Gruber observed, "The Greeks and the Romans after them believed that the four virtues are best understood as a composite unity. For example, it often takes courage to effect justice (as exemplified by Dr. Martin Luther King and Gandhi) and a courageous person is wise."

Aristotle in the *Nicomachean Ethics* indicated that courage was a balance between the vice of cowardice on one extreme and the vice of foolhardiness or recklessness on the other extreme. He believed that it was courageous to face fears, especially death in battle.

Courage and being courageous are mentioned thirty-five times in the Bible (New International Version). Believers are encouraged to "be strong and courageous." Courage is one of seven virtues of Bushido, the code of the Samurai warrior. Courage is also one of the virtues of Islam identified in the Qur'an—"And whoever is patient and forgiving, these most surely are actions due to courage."

Courage is richly documented in countless histories, biographies, and autobiographies. There are books that discuss *The Mystery of Courage* (Miller), *The Anatomy of Courage* (Moran), *Profiles in Courage* (Kennedy), *Why Courage Matters* (McCain and Salter), *The Courage to Be* (Tillich), *The Courage to Laugh* (Klein) and the like.

Courage remains a principal theme of literature— for example, Homer's *Iliad, Beowulf,* Shakespeare's *Henry V,* Victor Hugo's *Ninety-Three,* Charles Dickens' *Tale of Two Cities,* Erich Maria Remarque's *All Quiet on the Western Front,* Ayn Rand's *Atlas Shrugged,* Richard McKenna's *The Sand Pebbles,* James Clavell's *Shogun,* and Naomi Kryske's *The Witness.* More than one person has been encouraged by the exploits of a fictional character.

> **"Courage is a moral quality; it is not a chance gift of nature like an aptitude for games. It is a cold choice between two alternatives, the fixed resolve not to quit; an act of renunciation which must be made not once but many times by the power of the will. Courage is will power."**
>
> **Lord Moran**

Lord Moran (formerly Sir Charles McMoran Wilson) was Winston Churchill's personal physician during the

Second World War. During the First World War, he was a medical officer serving amid the mayhem and madness of trench warfare on the Western front. Lord Moran had ample opportunity to witness the effects of war and fear on men.

Lord Moran believed "a man's courage is his capital and he is always spending." He further believed that "no man had an unlimited stock of it." Courage would be used up by sustained exposure to physical danger and "discouraging circumstances." He likened courage to withdrawing money from a bank account. Once the funds were exhausted, no more withdrawals could be made. The person would no longer be able to be courageous.

> **"Standing up for what we think is right is not easy, but it may well get easier if we cultivate the habit of doing so."**
> **William Ian Miller**

Dr. William Ian Miller claimed that the U. S. Army's year-in-country rule for Vietnam combat tours was predicated on the bank-account depletion model of courage. Miller, however, made a critical distinction. He maintains, "Physical courage decays under intense and relentless demands of combat while moral courage … grows by the doing of deeds that require its mobilization."

The nature of courage is so dynamically diverse that we often miss a kernel of truth about it. Dr. Paul L. Escamilla cites novelist John Ames' belief that "there must be a prevenient courage that allows us to be brave." Escamilla notes that people are predisposed to being courageous because of their heritage—"the courage of our mothers, fathers, teachers, friends, heroes ancient and modern ... who, visibly or invisibly, walk with us into the various choice-making wildernesses of our lives...." This alone should be comforting news that all of us have the capacity to be courageous.

Summary of Key Points

- "Courage is the ability to confront fear, pain, danger, risk, uncertainty, and intimidation."
- "Physical courage is courage in the face of physical pain, hardship, or threat of death."
- "Moral courage is the courage to act rightly in the face of popular opposition, shame, scandal, or discouragement."
- Courage "is will power."
- Physical courage may "decay" after repeated exposure to life-and-death situations.
- Moral courage may grow when a person is engaged in actions concerning his moral stand.
- Courage is the key ingredient in transforming both our lives and the world.
- All people have the capacity to be courageous.

2

Acts of Courage

Courage is the spark that makes our humanness significant. Courage can take different forms. It can reside in the physical, intellectual, emotional, or spiritual domains as well as a combination of those four areas. Because of this, it is often difficult to categorize courage. Courage simply does not fit into neatly-sorted bins. While it's hard to define, people tend to know it when they see it.

Military history, as well as contemporary wars, is replete with examples of desperate battles and courageous warriors on both sides of an engagement. Walk through any of the cathedrals of courage— Gettysburg, Normandy, the Somme, Guadalcanal, or Shanksville, PA—and you will feel the ghosts of battles past brush against your face. It's a sobering and reverent experience.

Genuine courage is easily discerned. Facing another day as a combat soldier in Iraq or Afghanistan is an inspiring act of courage, as is the wounded veteran coping with his or her disabilities. Law enforcement officers in this country need guts to root out criminals and preserve public order and safety. The Bobbies of the London Metropolitan Police Service still courageously patrol the streets unarmed.

War causes a most intense interplay of emotions, so it appears logical to extend the lessons learned from combat to other fields such as business or sports. Caution, however, needs to be exercised. There are limits as to how far the military paradigm can and should be applied to non-military scenarios.

Not every act of courage involves a mortally-dangerous struggle. Small acts of courage occur every day. The child who protects a younger sibling from a bully is acting courageously. The high school student who refuses to give into peer pressure and cheat on a test or use drugs is acting courageously. The young man who conquers a fear of water and learns to swim is acting courageously. The young mother who braves a stormy night to get medicine for her sick child is acting courageously. The man who travels to a different city to look for work is acting courageously. Courage is a common act that makes people do uncommon deeds.

Some claim that virtually every human act involves some degree of courage. This belief dilutes and trivializes courage. Fortunately, there is no yardstick by which courage can be measured. There is no absolute scale going from "being afraid of one's own shadow" at the bottom to superhero at the top.

It is not our place to judge whether an act is courageous or not. What may require courage for one person may not be an act of courage for another. Some people feel comfortable speaking before a group of people. Others are terrified at the prospect. The good news is that the terrified person can work to overcome fear and become a confident speaker.

> "To be courageous requires no exceptional qualifications, no magic formula, no special combination of time, place, and circumstances. It is an opportunity that sooner or later is presented to us all."
> John F. Kennedy

All human beings have the potential to think, feel, and act courageously! That does not mean that we exhibit courage in everything we do. That also does not mean that we will be courageous in every instance or for every situation. A big-league ballplayer has the capacity to get a hit every time he comes up for bat, but it doesn't mean he will. He may strike out, line out, fly out, walk, or get hit by a pitch.

While each of us may strive to act with courage, the reality is that we sometimes fall short of our expectations both at work and at home. If each of us can just increase those times when we act with courage, we will discover a richness of new possibilities that will dramatically transform our lives and those around us. A little bit of courage goes a long way!

There appears to be a myth that physically courageous people are loud, brash, and devoid of fear. Elite special forces units such as the Green Berets, Navy SEALs, Britain's Special Boat Service and Special Air Service are often regarded in this way. So are naval aviators as popularized by the movie, *Top Gun*. This is a misconception. Most of these individuals would admit being afraid on occasion, but most would credit their discipline and high level of training for their success.

> "If we take the generally accepted definition of bravery as being a quality which knows no fear, I have never seen a brave man. All men are frightened. The more intelligent they are, the more they are frightened. The courageous man is the man who forces himself, in spite of his fear, to carry on."
> General George S. Patton, Jr., U.S. Army

At a Winston Churchill Leadership Symposium on the *Queen Mary* in 2001, I shared the speaking platform with a number of Churchill experts and scholars. Retired Admiral James Stockdale was there to speak on courage. This warrior scholar earned the Congressional Medal of Honor for refusing to compromise his principles while he was one of the senior prisoners of war in Vietnam. He was in captivity for over seven years. It was hard to believe that the white-haired, quiet-spoken gentleman with deep blue eyes was a bold attack pilot as well as a defiant prisoner. Admiral Stockdale was a man of great physical and moral courage.

Other professions require physical courage, too. A baseball player who steps into the batting box needs courage. Many Major Leaguers admit that having a pitcher hurl a 100-mph ball at them is unnerving. Or consider a quarterback who decides to run the ball knowing that over a ton of highly determined men are trying to tackle him.

> "I wanted you to see what real courage is, instead of getting the idea that courage is a man with a gun in his hand. It's when you know you're licked before you begin but you begin anyway and you see it through no matter what."
> Harper Lee

Serving on commercial fishing vessels surrounded by mountainous seas is perilous. So is working in a steel mill where thundering noises and tremendous heat add to the inherent levels of danger. In war zones civilian truck drivers, healthcare volunteers, and missionaries are frequently exposed to life-threatening situations. Journalists and combat cameramen covering world hot spots are under constant danger. Many occupations call for physical courage.

Courage is not limited to just the battlefield or dangerous civilian jobs. Joyce Meyer observed there are also "battlefields of the mind," the domain of moral courage. Moral courage involves taking a particular stand. Dr. William Miller calls moral courage, "lonely courage." He further believes that moral courage involves "calling attention to yourself or running the risk of being singled out in an unpleasant and painful way."

British poet and author Siegfried Sassoon served with distinction during his tour on the Western Front. He eventually became appalled with the senseless slaughter in the trenches and transformed into a vocal critic of the war.

Trench warfare on World War I was especially cruel and arduous. Hundreds of thousands of casualties were incurred by each of the major combatants during the Somme campaign alone in which the twenty-mile front advanced or retreated typically less than five miles (sometimes only hundreds of yards) during just over five months of fighting. Men died at twice the rate experienced during World War II. Almost an entire generation of Englishmen, Frenchmen, Germans—over three million men—perished (and twice that number were wounded) on the Western Front alone.

Sassoon's heroism on the battlefield took physical courage and his anti-war stand while still in uniform took moral courage.

Mahatma Gandhi led the people in the Indian subcontinent to oppose British domination and assert their right of independence between 1918 and 1947. His method of passive resistance entailed nonviolence and mass civil disobedience. Gandhi exemplified great moral courage. He remained faithful to seeking the truth and acting in a nonviolent manner despite great political, economic, and military pressures directed against his movement. Gandhi also displayed physical courage throughout his life. Many of his views were tremendously unpopular with the British, neighboring Pakistan, and within his own Hindu community (a member of which assassinated Gandhi in 1948).

Dr. Martin Luther King was greatly influenced by Gandhi's example. This Baptist minister became one of the preeminent leaders of the American civil rights movement. His political activism occurred during one of the most volatile periods of American history.

Between 1955 and 1968, Dr. King spoke with an eloquence and fervor rarely seen. He remained committed to his ideals of social justice for all Americans despite death threats, incarcerations, and racial violence. Like Gandhi, he was both physically and morally courageous, and he met a tragic death at the hands of an assassin's bullet in 1968.

> "Courage and cowardice are antithetical. Courage is an inner resolution to go forward in spite of obstacles and frightening situations; cowardice is a submissive surrender to circumstance. Courage breeds creative self-affirmation; cowardice produces destructive self-abnegation. Courage faces fear and thereby masters it; cowardice represses fear and is thereby mastered by it. Courageous people never lose the zest for living even though their life situation is zestless; cowardly people, overwhelmed by the uncertainties of life, lose the will to live. We must constantly build dikes of courage to hold back the flood of fear."
>
> Dr. Martin Luther King, Jr.

David Hackworth was an outspoken, two-fisted, straight-shooting, victory-oriented warrior. He served in the U.S. Army from the end of World War II until 1971. He spent three years in combat in Korea and five in Vietnam. He earned over ninety decorations including two Distinguished Service Crosses, ten Silver Stars, eight Bronze Stars, and eight Purple Hearts. He was considered a good candidate for the Congressional Medal of Honor twice.

Colonel Hackworth knew what it took to lead men in combat. He had transformed one of the worst performing units in Vietnam into one the most effective fighting teams of the entire war.

> **"Bravery is being the only one who knows you're afraid."**
> **Colonel David Hackworth, U.S. Army**

After his military service, Hackworth became a war correspondent and an advocate for the rank-and-file soldiers, sailors, and airmen. He understood the distinction between being a leader and a politician. Hackworth became a vocal critic of the huge military bureaucracy that was more concerned with its image than its performance. He opposed gold-plated and costly weapons systems that contributed little to the achievement of victory on the battlefield.

Although his advice was not followed in Vietnam, many of his prophecies became a reality. Colonel Hackworth was both physically and morally courageous. The former almost cost him his life countless times, and the latter earned him the scathing wrath and ridicule of Pentagon politicians.

What do Gandhi, King, and Hackworth have in common? They were men of integrity who would not accept the status quo. Rather than passively harbor their views, they took their causes onto the world stage. They endured hardships, criticism, and enmity for their stands. Their moral courage exposed each of them to physical danger. Hence we can discern the link between moral courage and physical courage: One frequently begets the other.

Courage is also boldly going where no person has gone before. Daniel Boone and Kit Carson, for example, both explored the savage wilderness of a newly developing nation. They defied scorching deserts, blinding blizzards, impenetrable mountains, lack of maps, determined hostiles, and uncertain food supplies. Like Christopher Columbus or Captain James Cook centuries before, they didn't know where they were going (or what they would find). When they got there, they didn't know where they were. And when they got back, they often didn't know where they had been!

Neil Armstrong and Buzz Aldrin probably had a better idea where they were going. Still, pioneers in time and space need courage to step outside the comfort zones of the present into exciting, new futures. Albert Einstein traveled outside the bounds of his contemporaries' imagination with his special and general theories of relativity. In the 1860's, the French impressionist painters—Pissarro, Monet, Manet, Sisley, Renoir, and others—abandoned the traditions and conventions of the past to look at the world in a new way.

> **"The real voyage of discovery consists not in seeking new landscapes, but in having new eyes."**
> **Marcel Proust**

But what about everyday people who display courage? Not everyone can be an explorer like Magellan or a scientist like Marie Curie (who won the Nobel Prize in Physics in 1903 and the Nobel Prize in Chemistry in 1911) or an artist like Picasso. Our awareness of displays of courage by ordinary people is usually limited to either what we've seen on TV, read in the newspaper, heard from co-workers or were examples of courage demonstrated by family and friends.

People sometimes have to step into new "worlds." Two of my sons, one who taught English to Japanese adults and youngsters and the other an IT analyst and trainer, spent extensive periods in Japan although neither of them had any previous exposure to Japan. Both needed the courage to live and work in a culture that was totally unfamiliar to them.

> **"Courage is being scared to death and saddling up anyway."**
> **John Wayne**

There are, however, other variations of courage that are needed to work through life's hardships. For example, Pats, my mother-in-law, was 87 when she moved from her Houston home of 51 years to Durham, North Carolina. Her husband of over 58 years had died three years earlier. She felt she could no longer run her home by herself and decided to move into an assisted living facility near her youngest son. She gave up long-time friends, support groups, and most of her household possessions. It was a heart-wrenching and frightening moment as she sat in the back of my car driving away from her home. But Pats courageously faced the future and never looked back.

Creating a new business, especially one that embarks on a journey into unknown territory, takes courage. While enduring a parking lot of cars during his commute from Newport Beach to Los Angeles in 1973, my friend, Duvall Y. Hecht, devised a way to fight the boredom of stalled traffic. His new business, Books on Tape, Inc., produced unabridged audio books which customers would rent by telephone (and later via the internet) and receive and return via mail. By the time he sold his business to Random House in 2001, he had 6,000 unabridged audio books. (In 1997 Reed Hastings' NetFlix apparently used a variation of the Books on Tape model and has been tremendously successful in bringing a wide selection of movies to over seven million subscribers.)

> **"To do the thing you think you cannot do—that's courage."**
> **Eleanor Roosevelt**

My mother, Annette, got her first computer when she was seventy-five and overcame a fear of failure in learning to use this new technological tool. She has been sending e-mails and surfing the web ever since.

It takes courage to do something you've never done before. Filmmaker Steven Spielberg observed that being creative often brings up fears and insecurities. Everyday, people in every walk of life do things that are new for them.

My wife, Naomi, recently put the finishing touches on her first novel, *The Witness*. She has worked over 4,500 hours during the past 36 months to produce a 600-page novel of fear, pain, hope, and love set in London. For a quiet, thoughtful person who believed she had little to say, this endeavour has been a powerful example of stepping out of one's comfort zone!

The examples of family and friends are not intended to equate with actions of soldiers on the battlefield. The fears and the costs are significantly greater in a combat zone. Courage, however, is required both on the battlefield and on the home front.

It is worth noting the feelings of people who act courageously. Some experienced stark fear. Others felt exhilaration or possibly anger. Many had a driving determination to act. Still others had an adrenaline-fueled high. Other people reported that it was the necessity of doing what had to be done that caused them to act with courage. And there were those who were not aware of any sensations while they were engaged in courageous acts. After the event, their feelings surfaced.

Courage is needed when a person:

- Exposes himself or herself to physical danger.
- Takes an unpopular stand.
- Refuses to compromise one's integrity, honor, values, principles, beliefs, etc.
- Confronts fear by taking action.
- Goes where no person has ever gone before.
- Does something that he or she has never done before.

When we look at the list above, we can see that courage is indeed a fundamental quality of both leadership and character. With courage, the seemingly impossible can become possible. What new, extraordinary things would become possible if you, your family, your team, your organization, your city, your state, your nation, or your planet exercised more courage?

Summary of Key Points

- Genuine courage is easily discerned.
- Courage need not always be a life-or-death struggle.
- Moral courage often begets physical courage
- Courage is a fundamental quality of both leadership and character.

3

Why People are Courageous

Don't let anyone sugarcoat this reality: Sacrifices are associated with being courageous. If there is no cost associated with an act, then courage is probably not involved. For example, eating lunch does not involve courage, nor does walking outside and picking up the newspaper. Clearly, every action we take does not involve courage.

Courage is costly! Some of the things courage might cost us include:

- Our friends
- Our money
- Our job
- Our time
- Our contentment
- Our influence
- Our life

The signers of the Declaration of Independence mutually pledged their lives, fortunes, and sacred honor.

Some lost all these things by signing that fundamental document of American liberty.

If courage is so costly, why are people courageous? Why does that ballplayer step into the batting box knowing that he may be hit by a Nolan Ryan pitch? He wants to help his team win the game. Why does a fire-fighter race into a burning inferno? He wants to rescue the occupants. Why does a police officer pursue an armed suspect? He wants to protect others. Why does a salesman make additional cold calls at the end of a long day? He wants to support his family.

If courage just had negative consequences associated with it, why would anyone be courageous? The positive attributes must overweigh the negative ones when someone acts with courage. Some of the things we might gain by being courageous are:

- Confidence
- Self-esteem
- Peace of mind
- Character
- Success
- Victory
- Love
- Joy
- Safety
- Security
- Honor
- Freedom
- Justice

- Loyalty
- Peace
- Respect
- Trust
- Wealth/Abundance

Courage is a tool, a means to an end. People are not courageous for the sake of being courageous. Rather, they are courageous because they feel compelled to achieve some desired outcome or result. Courage is an intermediary step between having a vision or goal in mind and following through with determination until that goal is accomplished. Courage may be the critical step in this process, but remains only a means to achieving some end.

Albert Schweitzer once spoke of "investing one's humanity." Each of us can uniquely and generously devote our time, our talent, our treasure, and our touch. Love may be the common element of these four actions.

Love is a powerful motivator. It can cause us to act despite fears and some significant personal cost. While love is not the complete answer to why people are courageous, it can certainly be one of the most sublime.

Senator John McCain who endured five years of captivity as a POW during the Vietnam War noted, "Love makes courage necessary. And it's love that makes courage possible for all of us to possess. You get courage by loving something more than your own well-being." Interestingly, both love and courage are symbolically represented by a heart.

> "Courage is generosity
> of the highest order."
> Charles Caleb Colton

Summary of Key Points

- The necessary conditions for courage to exist are the presence of fear and a cost for taking some action.
- Courage is a tool, a means to an end.
- There are many possible reasons why people are courageous, but love is one of the key factors.

4

The Five Cornerstones of Courage™

One of the most celebrated stories of courage involved a young, ruddy-faced shepherd. His opponent was a battle-hardened warrior almost ten feet tall. David was too small to use King Saul's armor, helmet, or sword that was offered to him. Instead he took only his staff, five smooth stones he picked up in the nearby stream, and his sling. With divine confidence he ran quickly toward Goliath and slew him.

It is not a coincidence that there are also five principles about courage that can help each of us slay the giants who defiantly confront our lives. The Five Cornerstones of Courage™ define the depth and breadth of courage. Once we understand the realities of courage, we can use strategies that can help us cultivate the courage that already exists inside us.

The Five Cornerstones of Courage are not silver bullets that will protect us from harm and evil. Despite thousands of years of searching for just such special powers, none have ever been found. Men and women were, however, not given a spirit of fear. Each of us was given the capacity to be courageous.

Think back to the time when you learned to ride a bicycle. Do you remember the fear you initially experienced? My first bike was a fire-engine red, 24-inch Schwinn with foot brakes. My feet didn't even touch the ground when I sat on it!

Everyone who has mastered riding a bicycle has stood at this crossroad. One road led to giving into fear and abandoning the new skill. The other road led to conquering the fear inside and overcoming the challenge. And once we mastered the distinction called balance, we took it for granted. We learned that riding a bicycle was fun and we could multitask while riding—riding with no hands, riding while eating a Popsicle, riding while talking to a friend, and more.

When we practice the techniques associated with each of the Five Cornerstones of Courage, we are preparing ourselves to respond with courage when the time comes.

Summary of Key Points

- **The Five Cornerstones of Courage define the depth and breadth of courage.**

5

The Nature of Fear

Humans are fearful creatures. Fear manifests itself in many ways. Below is a listing of some of the most common fears people have:

- Fear of failure
- Fear of success
- Fear of embarrassment
- Fear of ridicule
- Fear of loss
- Fear of rejection
- Fear of disgrace
- Fear of making a mistake
- Fear of public speaking
- Fear of going to the dentist
- Fear of pain
- Fear of death
- Fear of spiders
- Fear of snakes

- Fear of losing control
- Fear of responsibility
- Fear of heights
- Fear of aging
- Fear of being fired
- Fear of bad news
- Fear of a heart attack
- Fear of terrorism
- Fear of change
- Fear of the unknown

> **"Keep your fears to yourself,
> but share your courage with others."**
> **Robert Louis Stevenson**

In each industry there are specific fears associated with it. When I presented a leadership program to a group of real estate owners and brokers, their fears involved: maintaining their reputation, taking risks, having to terminate nonperforming agents, incorporating new methods, asking for appropriate compensation, and failing to run a business. On another occasion I worked with private mental health providers. Their specific fears involved financial survival, legal liabilities, changes to government regulations, government audits and surveys, and being able to run a business successfully. People are often more afraid of losing what they have than of not getting what they want.

In the food service industry courage plays an interesting role in confronting the fear of pain. My son, Kyle, a chef who has been cooking since the 10th grade, noted that "all chefs were once a typical line cook. All line cooks get burned or cut in one way or another. When it is a busy night, cooks get burned and you just have to put that aside and get the job done. Pain is more of a mental issue in a kitchen because it is unavoidable."

Many sales people tend to fear making cold calls, not reaching their weekly or monthly quotas, being rejected by the prospective client, making a sales presentation to a large group of potential customers, and asking for the sale. Trade association boards of directors often fear falling membership, decreased revenue, flat budgets, difficult board members, and not achieving association strategic objectives.

> "Courage is the triumph of mind and muscle over a natural urge to run away. The weakest creature will exhibit courage when cornered. The brave man doesn't wait to be cornered. A man has to have the stamina to 'take it' from the beginning, for when courage is routed, fear spreads as quickly as suddenly released steam."
> **Rear Admiral Harley F. Cope, U.S. Navy**

Fear is a powerful force. It greatly influences how we think, feel, and act. Consider how terrorists, for example, attempt to use fear to influence how we live our lives. And their threats have new weight as the result of their past acts.

Fear is a primary emotion. Therefore, fear may be disguised by secondary emotions that sit ahead of them in our behaviors. Worry, anger, frustration, nervousness, dread, apprehension, and uneasiness are examples of secondary emotions that may be sourced by fear. Thus, when we feel threatened, we experience fear in the form of these secondary emotions.

In her novel, *The Witness*, my wife, Naomi, noted that President Franklin Roosevelt spoke of the freedom from fear. She observed that this means we have the freedom to exercise other qualities such as love, generosity, or kindness. Freedom from fear also means we have the freedom to exercise courage because we're able to act despite the presence of fear. Fear no longer can dictate how we will act although it may still occupy our feelings.

> **The only thing we have to fear is fear itself—nameless, unreasoning, unjustified terror which paralyzes needed efforts to convert retreat into advance."**
> **Franklin Delano Roosevelt**

None of us performs at our best when fear completely dominates a situation. A constant diet of strong fears erodes our capacity to function mentally and physically. We know this from extensive reports about soldiers with prolonged exposure to life and death situations.

Colonel (later Brigadier General) Stephen G. Warren, USMC (Ret.) was the Commanding Officer of the Navy ROTC Unit at UCLA while I was a midshipman. He served as a Marine fighter pilot during

World War II, Korea, and Vietnam. He told me that in combat warriors experience "a high degree of apprehension" but must not become scared. A scared person loses emotional control and becomes unable to respond appropriately.

The presence of some fear, however, may be essential to keep us alert, sharp, and on our toes. When we are too comfortable or complacent, we tend not to put out our best efforts. How many people at work run on cruise control when a more junior co-worker sitting in the next cubicle has an eye on their job?

Therefore, too much or too little fear is not healthy for us. We need to get a proper balance. Fear management techniques or better yet, courage-building techniques, can help us deal with some of the fears that plague us.

> ## "Never let the fear of striking out get in your way."
> ### George Herman "Babe" Ruth

How are fear and courage related? Fear is a necessary ingredient and must be present in some form in order for a person to have the opportunity to display courage. Therefore, if fear is not present, then a person's actions do not involve courage.

Summary of Key Points

- Humans are fearful creatures.
- Each industry has an array of specific fears.
- The presence of fear is the necessary ingredient in order for courage to be exhibited.
- Freedom from fear means we have the freedom to exercise courage and act despite the presence of fear.

6

The Perception of Fear

Fear is a perception we might have about some situation. Our thoughts translate into certain emotions which cause us to take certain actions. People behave the way they do based on the way they perceive their environment. Every one of us has some perception concerning the world around us. And every perception we have is vividly real to us. Unfortunately, while every perception we have is real, it may not reflect reality.

Let me give a concrete example. Once while grilling supper outdoors on my barbecue, I asked my son to go inside for the metal spatula that was in the kitchen drawer just to the right of the sink. After five minutes, I walked in and asked him, "Where's the spatula?"

He replied, "I can't find it! It's not in the drawer."

I opened the drawer and pointed to the spatula. "There it is, right in front!"

My son's perception was that the spatula wasn't there because he couldn't find it. In reality, it was right where I said it would be. Every perception is real, but it may not represent reality.

It's also possible for two people to observe the exact same information and derive different conclusions. Remember the classic picture that to some resembles an old woman and to others a young woman? This one picture yields two different but real perceptions. Which do you see?

Regardless of whether a fear we encounter is reality, we experience real physiological and psychological responses to it. Imagine you're sitting at home alone on a dark, stormy night. While watching television in your living room, you hear a strange noise coming from the kitchen. You might think there's an intruder. Your heart rate goes up, your mouth gets dry, and your hands get clammy. These are real responses to the noises you hear. If you worked up the courage to investigate the sounds, you might discover that some tree branches were brushing against the side of your home or your icemaker was making new cubes. Still, before you discovered the reality of the situation, your perceptions caused you to experience fear.

Some people have claimed that fear is actually an acronym for "false evidence appearing real." I disagree. Fear may or may not involve false evidence. A soldier serving in Iraq might fear being killed by an improvised explosive device because one destroyed the Humvee in his unit the day before. That's not false evidence! It's terrifyingly real!

In December, 1971, I wrote an article for the U.S. Naval Institute's *Proceedings* magazine entitled, "NROTC at UCLA: The Colors Still Fly." In it I documented the events surrounding the fight to keep the Navy ROTC program on the land-grant college of the University of California at Los Angeles. In May, 1970, the university was a seedbed of protest and dissent directed again the war in Vietnam. The invasion of Cambodia and the subsequent events at Kent State University exploded the emotions of the anti-war elements on the campus.

I remember there was concern for the safety of the midshipmen during their annual dress parade. The event was rescheduled to a Sunday in early June when most students would be studying for finals. At 1:01 AM on Friday, June 5th, a bomb exploded in the Navy ROTC wardroom. Fortunately, no one was present at the time. This act of domestic terrorism certainly escalated the intensity of the anti-war protests.

When the 200 midshipmen paraded onto the field two days later, we wondered what new volatile actions awaited us. We were apprehensive but committed to participating in the parade. Happily, the protests and bombing backfired for the campus militants. A cheering crowd of 4,000 joined Governor Ronald Reagan and actor John Wayne in praising the midshipmen for their poise under pressure and their willingness to serve their nation in a time of war.

FEAR
by General George S. Patton, Jr., U.S. Army

I am that dreadful, blighting thing,
Like rat holes to the flood.
Like rust that gnaws the faultless blade,
Like microbes to the blood.

I know no mercy and no truth,
The young I blight, the old I slay.
Regret stalks darkly in my wake,
And ignominy dogs my way.

Sometimes, in virtuous garb I rove,
With facile talk of easier way;
Seducing where I dare not rape,
Young manhood, from its honor's sway.

Again, in awesome guise I rush,
Stupendous, through the ranks of war,
Turning to water, with my gaze,
Hearts that, before, no foe could awe.

The maiden who has strayed from right,
To me must pay the mead of shame.
The patriot who betrays his trust,
To me must owe his tarnished name.

I spare no class, nor cult, nor creed,
My course is endless through the year.
I bow all heads and break all hearts,
All owe me homage—I am FEAR.

Fear is an important protective mechanism for each of us. It typically gives rise to one of three responses. It can cause us to stand up to whatever is causing the fear. This is referred to as the "fight" response. We may decide that discretion is the better part of valor and decide to run away from what is causing the fear. This is called the "flight" response. Or the fear may cause us to become paralyzed and unable to move. That is called the "freeze" response. Fight, flight, and freeze are all normal human responses to fear.

Summary of Key Points

- Every person's perception of fear is real, but it is not necessarily reality.
- Fear is a normal protective mechanism.
- Human responses to fear are fight, flight, or freeze.

7

Cornerstone No. 1:

Courage is taking action despite fear.

Exercising courage is something we do, not something we think about. The first cornerstone of courage is: **Courage is taking action despite fear**. It is important to make a critical distinction about taking action. Not every action we can take is appropriate. Thrill-seeking actions or other foolhardy behaviors don't hit the target. These are what Jon Krakauer would call "intrinsically irrational acts, a triumph of desire over sensibility." It isn't courageous to scale Mt. Everest without bottled oxygen. Appropriate responses for a given situation are necessary.

> ## "Action is the fundamental key to all success."
> **Pablo Picasso**

Courage is not about having good intentions. It's not something we just think about doing. William Barret Travis, Jim Bowie, and Davy Crockett didn't think it would suffice if they only thought about the best way to keep General Santa Anna's battle-proven troops from surging into Texas. All their thinking would have yielded nothing. No, they had to commit their dearest possessions—their liberty and their lives—to defending that crumbling San Antonio mission called the Alamo.

Courage is an action sport not a passive endeavor. It takes place on the playing field of life, not from the safety of the couch watching the actions of others. There are no substitutes or alternatives. We must do something—take some action.

Another important consideration is that the action takes place even though the fear may still be present. This is what makes courage the special quality that it is: We act despite fear.

> ## "Fear is what you feel.
> ## Courage is what you do."
> ### Naomi Kryske

Summary of Key Points

- **Courage is taking action despite fear.**
- **The actions must be appropriate for the situation.**
- **Fear is something you feel. Courage is something you do.**
- **Fear does not necessarily disappear when we get into action.**

8

Courage-Building Strategies

Humans by nature are frightened creatures, but they are also adaptable and have developed a variety of ways to cope with and manage fear. Courage-building techniques can often help to eliminate the fears we experience or they can subdue the fear sufficiently to allow us to think and act despite its presence. Let's look at several of these strategies:

1. Do the thing you fear and the fear goes away.

Repetition can often give us the confidence to confront our fears. When I was in the Cub Scouts, we had a wood-burning session during one of our den meetings. I had never used a wood-burning set before and was alarmed at the prospect of getting burned.

My mother must have mentioned my distress to my dad, because for my next birthday I received a wood-burning set. With a little patient instruction from my dad, I was able to master my fears and eventually became quite comfortable at wood burning.

I'm sure you have had similar experiences, perhaps involving riding a bicycle, learning to swim, driving a stick-shift car, speaking before a group of people, or making a cold call. Sometimes the fear goes away completely, but sometimes it remains at a manageable level.

Several of my naval aviator friends have told me that making a night trap (landing on an aircraft carrier at night) was something that they never quite got over. One who had made over 300 night traps told me he always shook whenever he landed on a carrier at night— but he did it. He was a retired rear admiral who had won the Navy Cross in Vietnam!

Perhaps one of the most dreaded things a person is asked to do is to speak in public. This fear oftentimes shows up higher on a list of most feared things than death. As a professional member of the National Speakers Association for the past eight years, I have seen hundreds of individuals who were initially terrified at speaking to a group. A majority of these individuals were able to make great progress through practice. A person can overcome his or her fear of speaking in public through discipline, practice, and an eagerness to master that fear.

2. Develop a tolerance to fear.

Repeated exposure to fearful situations can enable a person to perform his or her mission despite the presence of fear. In one of my first experiences in the Navy, I served as the gunnery and missile officer in a guided missile destroyer, *USS Parsons (DDG 33)*. We were assigned as one of the ships providing naval gunfire support to Army and Marine Corps units operating near Quang Tri in South Vietnam in June, 1972.

I was a little uneasy for my first NGFS missions but I had to remain focused and alert because we had an important function to perform. Men's lives ashore as well as on board the ship were at stake. The potential for life-threatening problems such as taking hostile fire from ashore or having an in-bore explosion of our 5-inch 54-caliber naval gun did not go away.

I also learned a cardinal rule of warfare: It's better to give than receive! Repeated missions gave me a confidence that I could be effective at my task. But I was aware that potentially dangerous problems were always lying in wait. Leaders must remain vigilant. Overconfidence in the presence of potential danger continues to kill and maim people.

"Never take counsel of your fears."
General Thomas Jonathon (Stonewall) Jackson

---

3. Teams and team cohesion.

Teams give an individual an environment where some fears can be managed. They provide a way for a group of individuals to identify with something greater than any one of them. Peer pressure and a desire to be part of a winning team can become a dominant influence in the presence of fear. The adage that there is strength in numbers applies.

Memoirs by combatants have suggested that soldiers who went over the top during World War I in the face of almost certain death did so not because of coercion by their officers or fear of disgracing their loved ones at home but rather for fear of letting down their comrades with whom they lived and suffered in the trenches.

Sports teams, military units, and process action teams in business are examples of goal-oriented, outcome-based groups that attempt to accomplish results that an individual cannot. History abounds with examples of teams who have overcome all the odds and achieved incredible victories.

Perhaps one of the most celebrated accounts of team cohesion was the defense of Rorke's Drift in Natal, South Africa in 1879. The events were captured in the 1964 movie, *Zulu*, staring Michael Caine. Some 4,500 well-trained Zulu warriors attacked a British supply base and hospital manned by 139 soldiers (30 of whom were incapacitated).

Hot lead and cold steel were the order of the day. After ten hours of desperate hand-to-hand fighting, the Zulus withdrew. The battle-weary Zulus lost some 370 men, the British 15. Virtually every defender of Rorke's Drift was wounded. Eleven Victoria Crosses (the British equivalent of the U.S. Congressional Medal of Honor) were awarded for the valiant defense.

Shakespeare understood teamwork and the power of teams when he wrote in *Henry V*, "We few, we happy few, we band of brothers." So did Admiral Lord Nelson, hero of the Battle of Trafalgar in 1805, and virtually every military unit and force for the past 5,000 years.

The camaraderie among members of military units and sports teams creates a momentum of its own. The bond that develops when the team experiences harrowing events endures as long as the participants remain alive. This was eloquently demonstrated by the HBO series, *Band of Brothers*, based on the book by Dr. Stephen Ambrose. In the last sequence of the series, the actual surviving members of E Company, 506th Regiment, 101st Airborne, men in their eighties, talked about their continuing devotion to each other.

4. Team rituals—huddles, songs, cheers, martial music, bagpipes, flags, uniforms, gestures, national anthems, and mutual encouragement.

Teams can use rituals, symbols, and uniforms to bolster their morale especially when confronting potentially frightening circumstances. These behaviors can be observed before and during sporting events, prior to combat units going out on patrol, and sometimes, but not often, in business. The word "encouragement" means to inspire with courage, spirit, or hope—all elements of driving back the flight or freeze responses to fear and stimulating the fight response.

Early in my tour in *USS Parsons*, we were preparing to go on a WBLC (that's Navy alphabet soup for waterborne logistic craft) patrol just north of the demilitarized zone that divided North and South Vietnam. The area was notorious for drawing hostile fire from North Vietnamese shore guns. My small arms gunner's mates were preparing our two .50 caliber Browning machine guns and laying out 10,000 rounds of ammo each. It looked like serious business. I recall taking all this in with a sense of growing apprehension. Then I looked up and saw the stars and stripes of our national ensign snapping out straight in the freshening breeze. Just seeing Old Glory made me feel stronger.

If you have ever served in the military, you would probably agree that hearing the National Anthem played at a sporting, civic, or memorial event causes you to

57

stand taller and feel the hairs on the back of your neck stand up. Hearing bagpipes playing "Amazing Grace" has a similar effect.

Songs and music played a role during the siege of the Alamo in 1836. Former U.S. Congressman Colonel David Crockett played his fiddle and John McGregor his bagpipes to raise the spirits of the beleaguered defenders.

Gestures have also played a role in encouraging people. In 1415 during the Hundred Years War, Henry V invaded France. His forces met the French at Agincourt. The French outnumbered the English by as much as six to one. The English longbow, nevertheless, proved to be the decisive weapon as the English decimated the French.

Actor and longbow historian, Robert Hardy, maintains that the French taunted the English before the battle and threatened to cut off the bow fingers of the English if they didn't surrender. The English replied by holding up two fingers. This gesture was later adopted during World War II by Winston Churchill as a sign of defiance.

5. Training and cross training.

Training is a highly effective fear management tactic. The repetition of various processes helps to make responses automatic especially during emergencies. Trained persons are not walking into unknown territory. The familiar can help to minimize the impact of fear.

The more realistic the training, the better equipped the trainees will be to respond to the real thing. The Plano, Texas, Police Department has its officers run two to five miles before engaging in the shoot/don't shoot scenario training. They want their trainees fatigued to help them learn to function under pressure as they make life-and-death decisions involving the use of deadly force.

Dr. W. Edwards Deming, one of the founders of quality improvement, noted that most businesses do not do a very good job training their people. All too often, a new worker is given an inadequate amount of training, and this can lead to fear. One of Deming's 14 Points about business is to "drive out fear." Fear runs at cross purposes to productivity and profitability.

Training should not be regarded as a business expense but rather as an investment in the most important aspect of any business—its people. General Douglas MacArthur noted that training (led by capable officers) is what transforms a heterogeneous mass into a homogeneous group capable of achieving extraordinary results.

While training an employee for the work he or she will do is a good business practice, most businesses do not cross train their people in areas that are tangential to the immediate work of each individual. Cross training eliminates the indispensable man (or woman) syndrome. Fear of not being able to respond to an emergency often prevents key players in a business from taking a badly-needed vacation, taking time off for important family matters, or getting time to attend trade association conferences and training workshops.

> **"Courage is resistance to fear, mastery of fear—not absence of fear."**
> **Mark Twain**

Cross training enables a business to have a little more flexibility because the organization is not just one-deep in any critical positions. A cross-trained team is also better equipped to respond to situations where people might become casualties (e.g. the military, first responders—firefighters, law enforcement, medical, etc.). Businesses that consistently train and cross train their people are enhancing their productivity and profitability as well as driving fear out of the workplace.

6. Discipline.

Like training, developing discipline helps to reduce fear. Disciplined individuals can become conditioned to deal with new and unusual situations. Discipline in one area can often extend to another.

> **"O God of battles! steel my soldiers' hearts; / Possess them not with fear; take from them now / The sense of reckoning, if the opposed numbers / Pluck their hearts from them."**
> **Shakespeare, *Henry V***

In the military, marching and close-order drills for soldiers get recruits accustomed to following instructions delivered by higher authority. Being able to perform under pressure escalates during boot camp. Teamwork, cooperation, responsiveness, and other leader-follower relationships are interwoven under the umbrella of discipline. Physical and mental stress, exertion, discomfort, and hardships help to install the new habits of discipline. The maxim, "The more you bleed in peace, the less you bleed in war" is still valid.

In business, developing discipline will have to be tailored to the functions, responsibilities, and output products and services of the business. Discipline may take the form of answering the telephone in a prescribed manner or responding to customer complaints according to a well-defined process. Discipline involves the enforcement of previously established standards of behavior.

Disciplined individuals wear a form of armor that helps to insulate them from some fears. When the going gets tough, rather than falling apart, people can respond the way they were conditioned to respond. Even though extreme situations like war, natural and manmade disasters, and other calamities cannot be exactly duplicated, disciplined people can respond more effectively and are better equipped to survive those events.

7. Humor.

A wise man once said, "If you can keep your head when everyone about you are losing theirs, then you don't have a firm appreciation of the problem." Kipling did not say that—Master Chief Fire Controlman Doug Blair did. He was the senior enlisted person in *USS Parsons* and knew how to inject some humor into tense situations during operations on the gunline off Vietnam in 1972.

A well-placed joke, quip, movie line, or irreverent comment can often help others to keep their heads during stressful times. Just prior to the battle at Rorke's Drift, Private Fred Hitch, standing atop the provisions store house, shouted that he could see thousands of Zulus advancing toward them. Private Augustus Morris was reported to reply, "Is that all?"

The purposeful use of humor can divert attention, although perhaps ephemerally, from otherwise deathly serious circumstances. Allen Klein in his book, *The Courage to Laugh*, illuminated the importance of laughter to those who were facing death or dying of illness.

Every ship in which I served had a few men who by their humor or wit helped to relieve some of the tension of the moment. When fear thickly envelops a team, a good dose of humor is extremely beneficial. Otherwise fear can be terribly contagious and destructive to any team.

8. Comfort food.

Stress is often a byproduct of fear. Some people deal with stress and fear by consuming comfort food. Examples include: chocolate, peanut butter (that's mine), pizza, tuna noodle casserole (that's my wife's), a bowl of mac-and-cheese, or perhaps spaghetti with meatballs. Comfort food is fine in moderation, but continual overeating is not a healthy response to stress.

9. Self-encouragement, self-talk, visualization, affirmations.

Self-encouragement is a powerful way to deal with the uncertainties of upcoming events. We might intellectually tell ourselves that we are not afraid, but until we connect on an emotional and spiritual level, we probably do not believe it. Whistling in the dark only works if we think and feel it will work.

People have different rituals for psyching themselves up. Some listen to empowering music like the theme from *Rocky*. Some force themselves to get angry. Some slap their chests like a gorilla and shout. Some put themselves in a state where they feel powerful and unstoppable. Anthony Robbins, in his variations on NLP (Neuro Linguistic Programming), has some highly effective techniques for creating these state changes.

Some people prefer a less physical approach. When I started high school, I was initially overwhelmed by the difficulty of my classes. At the beginning of my first semester, I recall speaking to myself before I went to sleep. I told myself that this next semester would be a great adventure and that I could do it. I continued to do this at the beginning of each subsequent semester. I didn't know why I thought it would work, but it did. I graduated third out of a class of six-hundred-and-sixty.

How we speak to ourselves is another important aspect of building courage and managing fear. Most of us speak to ourselves more harshly than we do to our worst enemies. We can always find more negative attributes about ourselves than positive ones. Until we treat ourselves with respect and generosity, we cannot develop a healthy self-esteem. So choose to put yourself up, not down.

Visualization allows us to mentally create a picture of ourselves being successful in a certain situation. The more vivid and real we can imagine this picture, the better. Olympic skiers, for example, visualize their downhill runs with such clarity that scientists measuring the responses of their muscles can observe them firing off as they negotiate maneuvers downhill in their imagination. This process helps them to be mentally prepared before they ever strap on their skis. My best oil paintings were those that I thought about and painted in my mind long before ever putting any oil on the canvas.

Affirmations can be as simple as saying, "I think I can." We all read the book, *The Little Engine That Could*, when we were children. The moral of that book was to remain undaunted in the face of adversity. If we combine specific affirmations with actions that are later successful, we can internalize the beliefs and strengthen our ability to respond to future trials.

> "The courage of life is often a less dramatic spectacle than the courage of a final moment, but it is no less magnificent a mixture of triumph and tragedy. A man does what he must—in spite of personal consequences, in spite of obstacles and dangers and pressures—and that is the basis of all morality."
> John F. Kennedy

10. Prayer.

During difficult or fearful times, men and women have found tremendous comfort using prayer. Tapping into our spiritual domain and our faith can be a powerful antidote to fear. As the Apostle Paul wrote to his understudy, Timothy, "For God has not given us a spirit of fear and timidity, but of power and love and self discipline."

It bears mentioning that praying for courage may be answered instead by receiving circumstances that require the petitioner to be courageous. We learn by doing. We move forward by building on what we did and accomplished in the past. We need, however, to experience being courageous in our lives as opposed to understanding intellectually that courage is required. Courage is all about actions and doing.

Summary of Key Points

- Courage-building strategies help us to act despite persistent fears.
- Training and cross training may be the most effective courage building (and risk management) strategy for businesses.
- Discipline, humor, self talk, and prayer help people manage fears.
- Since we learn by doing, we need to experience being courageous instead of just understanding intellectually its nature.

9

The Inevitability of Risk

Risk is defined as the possibility of loss or injury as well as exposure to some peril, danger, or hazard. When a person is uncovered in these kinds of situations, a normal response is fear. Based on a person's fear threshold, one person's fun may be another's risk. (I wouldn't enjoy riding in a roller coaster with multiple inversions. Others relish the thrill.)

Risk assessment and risk management are prudent business practices. Such activities, when planned sufficiently on the front end of a project, will help minimize damage control efforts on the back end. Many times a business will devote more time, people, and capital to risk management than they do to opportunity management. The net effect of this is akin to driving down the road while looking through the car's rear view mirror.

People have different approaches to risk. Some people pursue, and in fact, enjoy taking risks. They can be called risk optimizers. Some people attempt to diminish the amount of risk they will encounter. They can be called risk reducers. Embedded in this category are those who may seek to transfer the risk to someone else as is done by purchasing insurance. Some individuals accept the nature of risks they encounter and can be called risk accepters. And some people will do everything they can to avoid taking any risks. They can be called risk avoiders.

Risk reduction or mitigation has seen a great resurgence. In former times risk was primarily associated with financial and legal exposure. Today risk is considered for virtually every aspect of a business, including information security, compliance with government regulations, supply chain management, technology innovation, business and political reputation, as well as responses to natural disasters and terrorism. Identifying the worst-case scenarios and developing appropriate responses help to lessen the impact of risk.

> ## "Success cannot be guaranteed.
> ## There are no safe battles."
> ### Winston S. Churchill

Risk is somewhat like stress. It is always present to some degree. The only people without stress, or any risks, are dead! Life is risky. Traffic lights, Food and Drug Administration testing of medicines, health department restaurant inspections, flu shots, incarceration of criminals, foreign treaties, over a million (city, state, and federal) laws in the U.S., and tens of thousands of other ways to protect life cannot guarantee any person a risk-free life.

Despite our best plans, there are always things that are not taken into consideration. Business executives, military officers, and people in every profession regularly deal with risk. To live means taking risks! Winston Churchill believed, "You have to run risks. There is a precipice on either side of you—a precipice of caution and a precipice of over daring."

Summary of Key Points

- Risks are inherent in life.
- The only risk-free people are dead.
- People must find appropriate ways to deal with risks.
- Despite our best plans, there are always elements or situations that are not taken into consideration.

10

Balanced
Risk-Taking Strategies

The key to living a joyful, productive, successful life is to take balanced or calculated risks. Aristotle believed that an individual needed to exercise sound judgment, weighing whether the benefits to be attained justified the underlying risks.

"Nothing is gained without some risk."
Louis L'Amour

There are a number of ways to take appropriate risks:

1. Exercise restraint/don't be impulsive.

A tractable balance needs to be found between reckless behavior on one extreme and excessive caution on the other. Since the parameters of business, leadership, and life are dynamic and ever changing, we need to adopt an analogous posture. Exercising restraint does not imply impassivity. Rather, it means evaluating the facts at hand, weighing trends, and anticipating likely changes in the wind. Restraint is an acquired taste like savoring fine wines. Developing a sensitive palate comes with experience. Risk management is similar.

Impulsive behavior can result in thrilling highs and catastrophic lows. And it doesn't allow us an opportunity to consider the risks adequately and reach an appropriate decision. When the outcome isn't what we desired, we may be forced to be a little more methodical and deliberate in our planning and subsequent actions. Prior prudent planning prevents poor performance.

2. Learn from mistakes.

No one wants to make a mistake, but isn't that how we develop good judgment? "To err is human, to forgive divine." If we don't have any negative outcomes from experiences, then perhaps we are being too cautious. We must also be able to discern well-intentioned actions from thoughtless behavior. George Santayana accurately observed, "Those who do not learn from the mistakes of the past are bound to repeat them."

"Be open, be honest, be generous. Leave enough room for people to fail, the only way any of us learns. Remember, every dog deserves two bites."
Duvall Y. Hecht

---

3. Embrace excellence not perfection.

When a person strives to be perfect, he may attempt to take as few risks as possible because he doesn't want to make a mistake. This ultimately becomes short-sighted since risk is an inherent reality of life. Unlike brain surgery or nuclear safety, most jobs do not demand perfection. Striving for it will cause a person to wait until everything is just right. Perfection will paralyze our performance and keep us from taking action.

Most professions are better served by adopting an attitude of excellence instead of perfection. Excellence is based on high standards of accuracy and quality but is not obsessed with achieving zero defects. Dr. Deming thought businesses should prevent errors on the front end of the product life cycle instead of doing 100% inspections on the finished product.

> ## "All life involves the management of risk, not its elimination."
> **Walter Wriston**

4. Don't attempt to control the uncontrollable.

In life some things we can control, some things we can only influence, and some things we can neither control nor influence. We need to ask the question: Are the events, situations, or people something that can be controlled, influenced, or neither controlled nor influenced?

71

Things that can *neither* be controlled *nor* influenced:

- Most people's reactions or behaviors
- The opinions and honesty of strangers
- World events
- The weather: hurricanes, tornadoes, earthquakes, tsunamis, ice storms, droughts, or heat waves
- Traffic congestion
- The price of gas
- The internet and its accessibility
- Airlines: when they will depart and whether your baggage will arrive with you
- The outcome of a baseball, football, or basketball game
- Governmental rules, regulations, and taxes
- The behavior of the stock market
- The day you die

> "We took risks, we knew we took them; things have come out against us ... Had we lived, I should have had a tale to tell of the hardihood, endurance, and courage of my companions which would have stirred the heart of every Englishman. These rough notes and our dead bodies must tell the tale..."
> **Captain Robert Falcon Scott, Royal Navy**

Things that *can* be influenced:

- The opinions of family or co-workers
- On occasion, other people's behavior
- The safety of your children
- Some events in which you are involved
- Your working environment
- The time it takes to get certain tasks done
- Your pet
- Your own personal success

Things that *can* be controlled:

- Your discretionary time
- How hard you will work
- Your thoughts
- Your emotions
- Your attitude
- Your tongue
- Who will be your friends
- Who will be your heroes
- Your personal commitments
- Your professional and personal affiliations
- Your spiritual journey
- Your discretionary money
- Your worries
- Your response to situations, events, and people

What is the common element in the "things that can be controlled" category? They all contain the word "your" or "you." We can only control things that involve ourselves, not someone or something else.

So where do we want to spend our time? Certainly we're not trying to control or influence things that are not controllable or able to be influenced. Wouldn't it be like trying to hold back the tide? Let's not waste our energy, that is, our thoughts, our feelings, and our actions, on things that we can't control or influence.

> "God grant me the serenity to accept the things I cannot change; courage to change the things I can; and wisdom to know the difference."
> **Reinhold Niebuhr**

5. Be open to new ideas and actions.

There are three domains involving knowledge. One domain can be called, "I know, I know." Each of us is an expert and maybe even an authority about a number of subjects. For example, I know I know about Winston Churchill, about driving a Navy destroyer around the ocean, and about leadership. Each of us has similar areas of expertise.

The second domain can be called, "I know, I don't know." For example I know I don't know about basket weaving—that is, I know it exists but I don't know how to do it. I know I don't know about Esperanto—I know it's a language but I can't speak it. I know I don't know about Ebola hemorrhagic fever —I know it exists but I don't know how to treat it. In a similar fashion, each of us has an awareness of a number of subjects but don't really know much about them. Surfing the internet has become a humbling experience where we learn how little we really know.

The third domain can be called, "I don't know that I don't know." This is the domain outside our personal awareness. It is an area of growth, extraordinary futures, and breakthrough results. If we could just tap into this domain, we could experience new possibilities in our lives.

Most of us spend our time in the first two domains that comprise our awareness. It is only when we look outside our own awareness that we can truly move to a new level of thinking and hence new actions.

How can we tap into the "I don't know that I don't know" region? We need to step outside our own personal awareness of the universe and converse with other people. This is why committed relationships with others are so valuable to our own growth and development.

> ## "The empires of the future are the empires of the mind."
> ### Winston S. Churchill

A personal example of operating in the third domain comes to mind. I served as Director of Security, Administration, Personnel, and Publishing at the Defense Nuclear Agency's Field Command in Albuquerque, New Mexico. Our overall mission was to ensure the safety, security, survivability, and surety of the U.S. nuclear stockpile worldwide. As my team worked to become even more effective, I learned about a ninety-year-old statistician who had new insights on how to attain higher quality. Attending Dr. Deming's week-long program on quality and productivity gave me new insights and completely changed the way my department thought about improving the hundreds of critical processes we managed.

6. Be persistent and tenacious.

A powerful risk-reduction strategy involves never giving up. Salespeople who consistently make cold calls despite the rejections are setting themselves up for success. In their view, persistence pays dividends, and not calling is far riskier than calling, in spite of the possible rejection.

7. Be ready to dance with changing circumstances—be resilient.

Nothing stays the same. The universe is always in a state of flux. We don't stay the same. We're either growing or decaying. Successful people roll with the punches. If they get knocked down, they stand back up.

My wife and I suffered catastrophic losses when Hurricane Katrina destroyed our home and office in Pascagoula on the Mississippi Gulf Coast. We lost virtually all our furniture, electric appliances, clothes, and over 3,000 books. Included in the loss were things that can never be replaced—photo albums, family recipes, musical scores, and keepsakes.

My wife and I had a choice. We could get bitter or we could get better. We chose the latter course. (See Chapter 19: Surviving a Calamity.) We needed to move forward with our lives and not wallow in pity as victims. We are certainly more sensitive now to people who have experienced great losses and hopefully can provide encouragement to them when we meet. I might add that the unexpected acts of generosity and compassion we experienced after the storm were overwhelming and miraculous!

8. Be nonjudgmental.

It's risky to defy conventional wisdom and be nonjudgmental about people and events. To judge others is a way of casting blame on them and absolving ourselves of any fault. The world looks for the person who will accept responsibility for his or her actions and not spin the facts to suit his or her ego. In fact it may be better to say nothing than to criticize or complain.

9. Be innovative in problem solving.

Every problem potentially has multiple solutions. Art teaches us this in an expressive way. There are many ways to portray a tree or a flower. Is one interpretation more valid than another? In life, there are many roads to achievement and fulfillment. We must not limit our approaches lest we become bored with life. The road less traveled may open up new possibilities.

Dr. Deming maintained that 85% of problems in business were process related and only 15% were people related. Yet the first place managers look when there is a problem is people. Perhaps the reason for jumping to conclusions is that the problem is not well defined.

Albert Einstein is credited as saying, "The significant problems we have cannot be solved at the same level of thinking with which we created them." Thus, problem solvers may have to understand the nature of their problem better before they can attempt to solve it.

Using Sakichi Toyoda's "Five Whys" approach can help us identify the real problem and its source or root cause. State the problem and ask why. Then take the answer and ask why again. Repeat the process as far as necessary to identify the source of the problem.

Separating the emotions from the problem can also be a challenge and a stumbling block to solving a problem. Reputation, pride, and ego often stand in the way of finding a solution. When I served on the Chief of Naval Operations staff in the Pentagon, I was exposed to some substantial egos. On one occasion a senior flag officer gave an incorrect answer to a technical question during a Congressional hearing. There is a simple and established process to correct these kinds of mistakes after a person gives his testimony. This flag officer refused to allow the correct information to be inserted in the Congressional Record. The end result: a highly successful program that had spent over $400 million of taxpayer money over the previous five years was stopped.

Branch Rickey, the innovative General Manager of the Brooklyn Dodgers, was among the first to use batting cages and helmets, pitching machines, a full-time spring training ball field, and statistics. Perhaps his greatest inspiration was to hire a former UCLA athlete and Army officer, Jackie Robinson. Robinson became the first black player in the Major Leagues in 1947 and won the Rookie of the Year Award that year. Two years later he was the National League MVP. Rickey's courageous decision to bring Robinson into the major leagues changed the course of baseball and sports.

The Container Store, a Dallas-based retail business started in 1978, believes that from a productivity point of view, "one great person equals three good people." Their motivated, enthusiastic, well-trained employees are allowed to use their intuition to help customers devise solutions to unique problems. By continuing to engage their customers in dialogue, they also enhance the likelihood of the customer doing business with them.

The Container Store's commitment to their customers and their employees reveals another sound leadership principle: give employees intellectual ownership in solving problems. By engaging employees' curiosity and intellect with new challenges, their turnover rate has typically been less than 15% per year, orders of magnitude less than what most retail businesses experience.

Being innovative is inherently risky, but it also helps manage the risk of running a business by enabling it to survive in a changing, global marketplace.

10. Don't be afraid to be vulnerable.

Any time a person does something creative, there will be others who will criticize the efforts. This is especially hard on new writers, artists, and musicians whose sense of self-worth may be extremely fragile. Baseball sportswriter Red Smith, the first sportswriter to win the Pulitzer Prize for Commentary, perhaps said it best: "There's nothing to writing. All you do is sit down at a typewriter and open a vein."

Imagine all the books, musical scores, and paintings that would not have enriched our lives if their creators hadn't risked being vulnerable!

79

> **"What would life be if we had
> no courage to attempt anything?"**
> Vincent van Gogh

Anyone who has done something new, such as Bill Gates, airship pioneer Hugo Eckener, impressionist painter Camille Pissarro, or nuclear submarine developer Hyman Rickover, was initially ridiculed. German philosopher Arthur Schopenhauer observed, "All truth passes through three stages. First, it is ridiculed. Second, it is violently opposed. Third, it is accepted as being self-evident." Therefore, if we can endure the capricious comments of those who neither create nor produce, a new panorama of possibility unfolds.

Courageous leaders realize that balanced risk taking modulates the inherently dangerous environments in which they operate. Since risks can neither be avoided nor should they be irresponsibly pursued, these leaders can use risk-reduction strategies to lower their exposure to losses and failure.

Summary of Key Points

- Balanced risk-reduction strategies can help us to respond appropriately.
- It is a waste to spend energy and time on things over which we have no control or influence.

11

Conquering Procrastination

Is the name Angelo Siciliano familiar? Angelo lived in New York in the 1920's. One day he and his girlfriend were sitting on the beach at Coney Island when something happened that would change his life forever. A bigger stronger man came by and kicked sand in Angelo's face. Unfortunately, Angelo was a ninety-seven-pound weakling and suffered the humiliation by doing nothing. He promised himself that he would never again have to experience the helplessness that comes from being physically weak.

Angelo didn't have the money to buy weights or join a gym, so he had to get more creative. He noticed that the big cats at the zoo frequently stretched so that one muscle group was pitted against another group. This gave him an idea. Angelo pushed his palms together and noticed that if he held them together forcefully for several seconds, his arm muscles were exercised. He developed a number of routines where one muscle group was put under tension by working against another.

Angelo practiced his exercises with a great deal of discipline, patience, and perseverance. Over time he noticed that he was getting stronger and his muscles were gaining definition. He called his body-building routine, "Dynamic Tension." Eventually Angelo became exceptionally well-developed and started to win various body-building contests. He eventually changed his name to Charles Atlas and became world famous for his strength and natural build.

One of Charles Atlas' feats of strength was to use a line (that's a rope for you landsmen) to pull a 73-ton railroad car some 120 feet. Such an action takes a great deal of muscle power, but Atlas also relied on the principle of inertia and momentum to assist him.

A physics book tells us that inertia is a fundamental property of matter. A body at rest will remain at rest or a body in motion will remain in motion unless acted upon by an external force. In the case of the railroad car, Atlas had to overcome the frictional forces and the force of gravity that held the car glued to the ground. If he could get the car to budge—even a little—he knew the car would move more easily. The car's momentum would then allow it to move slowly as long as Atlas pulled the line with more force than the forces acting on the railroad car's wheels.

Like Atlas, once we overcome the inertia of getting into action, we have a fighting chance of remaining in motion if we continue to be committed, consistent, and dedicated to our task. The first steps are always the hardest, so we need to get started, build momentum, and keep moving.

As a postscript to the Charles Atlas story, it really works! When my younger brother, Tom, was a teenager, he saw an ad for Charles Atlas' Dynamic Tension program in the back of *Popular Mechanics*. He sent away for it and dedicated himself to doing it every day. It wasn't long before he became extremely fit. It started him on a lifelong exercise regime that continued in the U.S. Marine Corps and the original Gold's Gym in Venice, California. His incredible strength today, some forty years later, is the direct result of Charles Atlas' body-building technology.

Procrastination: the Thief of Time

Now I'd really like to address procrastination—or perhaps we should do this section a little later. What do you think?

No, let's do it now! Conquering procrastination is a critical time management skill. Most people suffer from some degree of procrastination while others are paralyzed by it. It's easier to procrastinate and get a cup of coffee than make a cold call. It's easier to straighten up the paperclips in your desk drawer than to write a proposal for a customer. It's easier to go to an office supply store than to discipline an employee.

So why do we procrastinate? Sometimes we have to deal with a fear of failure or rejection or embarrassment. Maybe we have an underlying dislike for authority, especially for some authority figure during our youth— "I'll show him ..." Sometimes we are overwhelmed by too complex or unpleasant a situation. Sometimes we have too many competing demands on our time and we can't decide, so we do none of them. Sometimes we want everything to be absolutely perfect so we don't begin until we think we can achieve that kind of standard.

When we procrastinate, we unleash a whole spectrum of negative emotions such as fear, guilt, worry, hostility, depression. Procrastination has a cost, too. It costs us self-respect. It costs us clients and customers. It costs us market share. It costs us getting the jump on competitors. It costs us high corrective maintenance dollars when we could have been doing less expensive preventive maintenance on our equipment.

We have all experienced procrastination. How can we slay this dragon? Shouldn't we uncover the real identity of procrastination? Once we've unmasked its true nature, you might think differently about it. There is something insidious about procrastination that each person badly needs to know. Until we face up to the realities involving it, we may tend to just dismiss procrastination as some harmless human foible. Procrastination may be one of the greatest mental hurdles each of us faces on a daily basis.

Procrastination is a thief! It steals from each of us the most precious, nonrenewable resource there is: time! It diverts our attention from the important to the unimportant. The old saying, "Time is money," would be more accurate if we said, "Time is life!" All the wealth in the world cannot buy a dying man more time. As we get older, time seems to run faster and faster for us. The consequences of procrastination ultimately impact our lives. Procrastination is a thief that robs us of our lives!

When we postpone doing a task, we remain anxious and tense. Guilt dogs our heels. On the other hand, when we don't procrastinate, we give ourselves the satisfaction, relief, and freedom from anxiety that come from accomplishment.

Procrastination is directly linked to courage. Procrastinators may lack the courage to do what is necessary, but courageous people do not procrastinate!

Churchill recognized the importance of taking action. During the Second World War, he placed small red labels with the words "Action This Day" on the instructions and decision papers he sent to his staff. This helped create a sense of urgency that what the staff was doing was vitally important to the war effort. We, too, need a sense of urgency. Each day we need to take some actions regarding our careers, our lives, and our dreams.

If we want to conquer procrastination, then we need to get angry at it! Don't let it rob us of our lives! Keep moving toward your visions with courage!

We didn't learn to procrastinate overnight. Rather, we conditioned ourselves to respond to our environment by procrastinating. Procrastination has a binary quality. Either we do it or we don't. When we take back control of our time and our life, we must be bold! Bury procrastination before it buries us! A tragic story comes to mind.

Mattie was a courageous boy. At age three, he started writing poetry to help him cope with the death of his brother. Mattie had the same genetic disease. It affected his breathing, caused muscle weakness, and impaired most of his bodily functions.

Mattie was not unfamiliar with hospitals, blood transfusions, or feeding tubes, but he possessed a gift of seeing the artistic beauty that can exist in a person's heart. Despite Mattie's young age, he wrote poems that connected with people of all ages. *Heartsongs* and the four volumes that followed became best sellers. His poems were about his happiness, his pain, his dreams, his fears, and his hopes.

As Mattie's condition worsened, he remained upbeat, saying he didn't fear death. His work was full of life, a quest for peace, and a testimony of faith, hope, and love.

He said each person has an inner voice he called a "heartsong." "It's our inner beauty, our message, the song in our heart. It's our sense of why we are here and how we can keep going. It is like a purpose."

Mattie Stephanek's purpose was to spread peace, hope, and encouragement to the world. A rare form of muscular dystrophy claimed his life at thirteen, but the flame of his spirit still burns brightly in the hearts of those who have read his impassioned poems.

Mattie is a perfect example of someone who did not procrastinate. What's your heartsong? What's keeping your heartsong from burning brightly?

Summary of Key Points

- Since the first steps are always the hardest and most critical, get started, build momentum, and keep moving.
- Procrastination is a thief that steals our time, our productivity, our dreams, our vitality, and our lives.
- A sense of urgency is necessary to take back control of our lives.

12

Strategies to Beat Procrastination

Let's look at some practical strategies that will help us overcome the addiction of procrastination.

1. Commit to solving the problem.

Unless you are fully committed, you won't stop procrastinating. You cannot be partially committed. It's all or nothing!

2. Consider the cost of procrastinating.

What are the strategic, big picture consequences of procrastinating? Think about one thing (something that you could be, do, or have) that if you did, would significantly change the course of your life. For example, perhaps you want to become a published author. Now fill in your answer at the end of the sentence below:

PROCRASTINATION is a thief that robs the best of

_____ .

In our example you would have, "Procrastination is a thief that robs the best of authors." How does that answer make you feel concerning your specific dream?

3. Take back control!

What do you intend to do to take back control of your time so you can do what is crucial to you? Unless you get angry at what is stealing your destiny, you'll not be committed enough to put procrastination in its rightful place—the trash bin of behaviors you'll no longer practice.

4. Identify compelling reasons for not procrastinating.

What's the payoff for you? Can you identify 10, 20, or even 50 specific reasons why you must take back control? If you are unable to come up with a large number of reasons for not procrastinating, you are not genuinely dedicated to changing.

> ## "Do not let what you cannot do interfere with what you can do."
> ### John Wooden

5. Develop a "Do it NOW!" attitude.

While I was serving in the guided missile destroyer, *USS Goldsborough (DDG 20)*, homeported in Pearl Harbor, Hawaii, I was privileged to be second in command to the Commanding Officer, Commander Mike

Mullen. I spent hours with him every day witnessing how he led and motivated our 500+ officers and sailors.

Commander Mullen was an exceptional leader. His watchword was "Do it now!" I can't tell you how many times I heard, "Do it now!" I even started to tell my three children to "Do it now!" You can imagine how that went over.

"Do it now" creates a sense of urgency that pervades the fabric of a business' corporate culture. Without this reflex, neither leadership nor courage can function effectively.

Under Commander Mullen's courageous leadership, *Goldy* became one of the top-performing warships in the Pacific Fleet. Commander Mullen's career also blossomed. After *Goldy*, he commanded another warship and worked his way up through the admiral ranks to the most senior naval officer, the Chief of Naval Operations. Today, Admiral Mike Mullen is the Chairman, Joint Chiefs of Staff, the principal military advisor to the President and Secretary of Defense! "Do it now" certainly worked for him. It can work for each of us, too.

6. Set deadlines/make public promises.

When we finally commit to stop procrastinating, it's vital to obligate ourselves to this task and burn the bridges behind us. Set specific deadlines and tell other people. When will you start?

7. Divide and conquer the problem.

How do we eat a whale? We do it one bite at a time. The same principle applies to dealing with overwhelming and complex problems. Each challenging task can be broken down into smaller, more manageable segments. Perform bite-size pieces of the actions. Don't let anyone "super-size" your portions either!

8. Delegate when possible.

Delegation only works when there are sufficiently trained and cross-trained people. Outsourcing may be cost effective for some functions in a business, but there is no substitute for having your own people to provide leadership and innovative solutions to new challenges. As Dr. Richard W. Hamming observed, "If you don't have in-house ability, you tend to get outhouse results!"

In his book, *A Wind from the North: The Life of Henry the Navigator*, Ernle Bradford noted that a person can operate in space or in time. To operate in space uses more time and may not be the best use of it. Bradford used Portuguese Prince Henry to illustrate this premise. Had Henry operated in space and personally explored the coasts of Africa in the 1400s, he might not have achieved as much historical attention because sea voyages were inherently long, slow events. Instead, Henry operated in time by financing, motivating, and encouraging other explorers, navigators, and mapmakers who gave understanding and dimension to the West African coast.

The most important consideration involving delegation is that leaders can only delegate authority, not responsibility. A leader cannot pass the ultimate responsibility and accountability to someone else. Shared responsibility means no one is responsible. There must not be ambiguities like this, either on the battlefield or in the boardroom. A leader can allow others to work some of the problems for him by giving them certain authority, but the leader still retains ultimate responsibility.

Here are some other insights and strategies involving delegation:

- Delegation means using other people's time.

- Analyze the nature, scope, and outcomes you desire.

- Identify the right person: maturity, motivation, experience, technical expertise, amount of trust you have in him/her.

- Consider how you'll maintain control of the job *before* you delegate it.

- Determine how much authority will be delegated, such as gathering information, suggesting alternative solutions, making decisions, and reporting requirements.

- Don't allow sub delegation without prior approval.

- Establish reviews at regular intervals or critical milestones to track delegated tasks.

- Create a motivating, empowering, encouraging environment.

- Tell the person to whom you delegate "what," "why," and "when," not "how."

- Don't micromanage the plans and decisions of the person to whom you delegate.

- Ensure accountability and scrupulously. evaluate performance.

- Critique your battles and learn from mistakes.

9. Encourage yourself with positive self-talk.

It is human to be harder on ourse ves than on others. However, show me a person who has not failed in some endeavor and I'll show you someone who has never taken a risk. Most major league baseball players fail about 70% of the time in their attempts to hit the ball. A .300 hitter is considered a valuable addition to any ball club. So let's hear a little positive chatter when you come up to bat!

10. Celebrate your successes.

When you get a hit, or better yet a home run, don't forget to celebrate your success. These celebrations may be private or public as necessary. The public ones may serve as encouragement to others to model desired behaviors or similar achievements.

We owe it to ourselves to install in a permanent way new behaviors when we overcome negative habits like procrastination. Our brains will form new neural pathways for success when we encourage subsequent positive behaviors.

11. 7-17-27 Stairstep Approach™

The key to conquering procrastination is just to *get started!* This methodology is designed to minimize the fears, real or imagined, associated with tackling a project. Everyone can commit to small bite-size pieces of work involved in a large, imposing project. (If it is only a small project that is being put off, the problem is not procrastination but laziness!)

7-17-27 Stairstep Approach™

1. Identify a project that causes you to procrastinate.

2. Commit to working on the project for 7 minutes and then do so.

3. Briefly stop, and then immediately recommit to work for 17 minutes and do so.

4. Finally, briefly stop, and immediately recommit to work for 27 minutes and do so.

5. Now stop and celebrate that you just spent 51 minutes at a task that you'd been putting off!

6. Repeat the 7-17-27 process again and again. You're now on your way toward getting the job done.

"Somebody should tell us right at the start of our lives that we are dying. Then we might live life to the limit, every minute of every day. There are only so many tomorrows."
Michael Landon

Get started, build momentum, and keep moving. There's one big false assumption involving procrastination: that you're not going to run out of time. Remember Mattie? He didn't have any time to waste. Do you?

Summary of Key Points

- Develop a "do it now" attitude.
- Leaders can only delegate authority, not responsibility.
- The 7-17-27 Stairstep Approach™ is a practical way to get started and keeping moving.
- It's possible that our procrastination in the past has created an unsolvable problem because we will run out of time.

13

Cornerstone No. 2:

Courage grows out of clarity of purpose.

Introspection is the examination of one's own thoughts and feelings. In order to cultivate courage in our lives, we need to be extremely clear about:

- Who we are
- What we stand for
- What we value
- What we are prepared to do

It is easy to be deceived by the opinions of others or even the false masks we wear to influence those opinions. Clarity of purpose is a house whose foundation is constructed on bedrock not sand.

The second cornerstone of courage is: **Courage grows out of clarity of purpose.** Our actions, however, speak louder than our thoughts and intentions. When our actions are congruent with our thoughts and values, then we will experience a purposeful life without shame.

When the going gets tough, tough-minded individuals get going. Remember, "It's not the size of the dog in the fight but the fight in the dog." Mental toughness is another way of saying we are disciplined and have clarity of purpose based on our values.

If a person values generosity, wouldn't he be likely to reach out to help a stranger? If a person values loyalty, wouldn't such a person stand up for a team member? If a person values moderation, might this person avoid excessive behavior? In each of these cases having a clear sense of purpose enables the person to be courageous with respect to honoring his or her values.

"Crisis often creates clarity."
Dr. Paul L. Escamilla

The greater one's clarity of purpose, the more able one will be able to find the inner strength necessary to face fearful situations with courage, especially moral courage! This is especially true in instances where survival is in jeopardy. On the other hand, when a person is not clear about what he or she values, it is less likely that a person will stick out his or her neck and become involved in situations that require courage.

It is not the purpose of this book to help the reader develop his or her values. I will leave that up to the reader. Dr. Robert Schuller once observed, "If you don't stand for something, you'll fall for anything." Values are an anchor that keeps us grounded to what we hold most precious in our lives. It is also written, "For where your treasure is, there your heart will be also."

Some Qualities People Value

Acceptance	Friendship	Patience
Accountability	Generosity	Patriotism
Adventure	Gentleness	Peace
Appreciation	Goodness	Perfection
Balance	Happiness	Personal growth
Beauty	Helpfulness	Piety
Charity	Honesty	Power
Cleanliness	Honor	Privacy
Commitment	Hope	Prudence
Compassion	Hospitality	Respect
Competence	Humility	Responsibility
Courage	Humor	Restraint
Courtesy	Idealism	Self-control
Creativity	Imagination	Self-reliance
Curiosity	Individualism	Sensitivity
Democracy	Independence	Security
Dependability	Integrity	Serenity
Determination	Intuition	Service
Diligence	Joy	Sharing
Discipline	Justice	Sincerity
Education	Kindness	Sympathy
Empathy	Love	Tact
Endurance	Loyalty	Temperance
Enthusiasm	Magnanimity	Tenacity
Equality	Mercy	Thoughtfulness
Excellence	Moderation	Tolerance
Fairness	Modesty	Tradition
Faith	Morality	Trust
Fame	Nonviolence	Truth
Fidelity	Obedience	Understanding
Forgiveness	Openness	Wealth
Freedom	Optimism	Wisdom

"People who have the courage to face up to the ethical challenges in their daily lives, to remain faithful to sacred oaths, have a reservoir of strength from which to draw upon in times of great stress—in the heat of battle."
General Charles C. Krulak, U.S. Marine Corps

Moral courage, that is courage based on a person's convictions, conscience, values, or beliefs, springs from this second cornerstone of courage. The strength of one's courage is directly proportional to the strength of one's convictions. Ministers, missionaries, whistleblowers, social activists, ethical thinkers, and Holocaust survivors demonstrate moral courage. But they do not have a monopoly on it. Men and women serving in the military, civilians in government, physicians, attorneys, educators, and people in all professions are called upon to exercise moral courage.

"Never give in! Never give in! Never, never, never, never—in nothing great or small, large or petty—never give in except to convictions of honor and good sense."
Winston S. Churchill

People on both sides of a moral dilemma can be courageous. In addition ordinary people in every walk of life are called upon daily to act with integrity at work and home. These individuals are morally courageous in the face of a world that values power, prestige, possessions, popularity, and pleasure.

Dr. Hylan B. Lyon, Jr., a former naval aviator, was experienced with dangerous situations where courage and clear thinking were required. He noted, "I often think moral courage is something you observe but cannot predict." His expectations of how men would perform under stressful situations were often wide of the mark. This is because courage is a nonlinear event, with no smooth and continuous cause and effect relationship. He further confirmed this with his observation, "Some of the fabric of toughness that needs to be there when you are jumped by MIGs only surfaces during the encounter." This is the wildcard that prevents combat commanders from predicting with absolute certainty the outcome of a battle.

The second cornerstone of courage can give us strength when all else seems to be failing. Consider this example. Norman's doctors told him that he only had one chance in five hundred of recovering. Some unknown disease had left him virtually paralyzed from the neck down. He was also in excruciating pain. Norman refused to be a passive observer. He made it clear to everyone that he'd be that one survivor.

Based on his own research, he knew that optimism, a positive attitude, and avoidance of panic were essential to any medical recovery. With his doctor's approval, he began an unusual therapy. He sent for films of the funniest television shows, hoping that laughter would boost his immune system and help his dire condition.

Norman discovered that laughter was indeed good medicine. Laughter plus some other unique medical approaches started to make a difference. Ten minutes of a real belly laugh would give him two hours of pain-free sleep. Within a few weeks, he could move his thumbs. Over several months his range of motion steadily improved. Eventually he improved enough to go back to work as an author and editor-in-chief of the *Saturday Review*, although his knees were still wobbly. Year by year he got better, and he did become pain free.

What was the secret of Norman Cousins' success? He had a purpose. Purpose is a filter through which a person looks at the world and his circumstances. This filter asks the question, "How can I use this information, situation, or resource to help me achieve the outcomes I desire?"

"Courage is the freedom to choose."
Norman Cousins

In Norman's case, he had an illness, and he was determined to beat it. His purpose was to survive. He saw everything through this particular filter.

There is an overarching belief that we can add depth and balance to our lives. Believers in continuous self-improvement seek to better themselves. They open themselves up to new ideas which may cause them to reexamine their values. Such examinations will either strengthen the values they hold or lead to replacing them with something else. Refining what we consider important is a way in which we can ensure we do not atrophy mentally.

Clarity of purpose enables us to be courageous when we don't think we possess courage. Having well-defined core values allow us the ability to prioritize what we do with our time, talents, treasure, and touch. Our priorities can be general in nature, such as putting one's family before business. Our priorities can also be specific in nature. In this arrangement they take the form of a goal or outcome such as Norman Cousins' desire to recover from his unknown disease. Clarity of purpose solidifies our courage.

> "The test of character is not 'hanging in' when you expect light at the end of the tunnel, but performance of duty and persistence of example when you know no light is coming."
> Admiral James B. Stockdale, U.S. Navy

Summary of Key Points

- Courage grows out of clarity of purpose.
- The clearer we are about what we value, the easier it will become to act with courage when the situation arises.
- "Moral courage is something you observe but cannot predict."
- Moral courage hinges on the strengths of one's convictions, values, and beliefs.
- Clarity of purpose solidifies our courage.

14

Focus and Concentration

Winston Churchill was known for his ability to focus on a task and not be distracted by peripheral diversions. His incredible productivity in writing 57 books, 1,600 magazine articles, and over 2,400 speeches—over 30 million words—was accomplished during 8 years in the military and 64 years in the House of Commons where he held 11 cabinet positions and was Prime Minister twice. That's concentration!

Louis L'Amour, the prolific western author of more than a hundred novels, said he could concentrate so well that he could write a novel anywhere. To prove his point, he once sat on a busy Hollywood street corner with his typewriter and worked on a book. A truck driver slowed down at the stoplight, and shouted out his window, "Hey, you must be Louis L'Amour!"

Clarity of purpose also means that we stand firm on our convictions. We don't let obstacles and adversity prevent us from carrying out our mission. Similarly, we keep our eye on the ball. Focus means not letting anything distract us from what we need to be doing. This implies being present to observe what is going on around us and allowing our conscience to evaluate our observations. (Don't neglect or ignore your peripheral vision while you're focusing intently on an objective. Maintain a 360° awareness to avoid being blindsided.)

Here are some techniques that will help us to focus and concentrate when we work:

- Have the right environment and atmosphere
- Reduce or minimize distractions
- Reduce noise
- Reduce clutter in your physical surroundings
- Reduce interruptions such as walk-ins, e-mails, telephone calls, meetings
- Work at your optimal time (e.g. some people are morning people, etc.)
- Challenging, interesting, or critically important work is more conducive to focus & concentration
- Follow the guidance, "Plan your flight and fly your plan"
- Maintain calm—don't be impulsive or hasty
- Boredom impedes focusing
- Postpone personal activities when focusing
- Emotional stress negatively impacts focusing
- Collaboration with the right people can have a positive effect
- Use the right technology
- As the inconvenience factor increases, the ability to focus decreases

- Blocks of time ensure that essential deliberations can be achieved

- The fun factor and celebrations of achieving milestones enhance focus

Focus implies a single-mindedness of interest or inclination. Intense laser-like focus illuminates one's values and minimizes peripheral distractions. When there is abundant drive and momentum created by our convictions, courageous acts proliferate.

Imagine boldly going where no person has gone before! Captain Kirk and Spock can certainly claim: "Been there, done that, got the tee-shirt!" And so could Norma.

Norma remembered at an early age having no interest in traditional female roles. Her father suggested she become an architect. That resonated with her soul, but she had no role model to follow. When Norma was growing up, architecture was dominated by men.

Most people in her situation work extremely hard, but in her case it took an inordinate effort. She completed Columbia University's School of Architecture and then looked for a job. Nineteen architectural firms turned her down, but the twentieth said yes. She continued to work hard to master her profession. In time she carved out an impressive record of successes. Among her designs are the US Embassy in Tokyo and Terminal One at Los Angeles International Airport.

Norma Sklarek pioneered the way for other women to enter the field of architecture. She'd tell students, "Do not give up on anything you find difficult." What makes Norma's story even more significant is that she became the first black woman to be licensed as an architect, the first to be to elected as a fellow of the American Institute of Architects, and the first to form her own architectural firm.

Norma never lost sight of her purpose. She needed to be courageous to become an architect. And she was.

Summary of Key Points

- The need to focus and concentrate on our challenges means we need to keep our eye on the ball.
- Intense laser-like focus illuminates one's values and helps to minimize peripheral distractions.
- To avoid sapping one's focus, maintain calm. Do not be impulsive or hasty.

15

Courage Feeds on Curiosity

An important corollary grows out of the second cornerstone: Courage feeds on curiosity. What propels explorers in time and space is an unquenchable desire to learn. The motivations of such explorers rest not with thrill-seeking adventure (although that might be one of the side benefits of exploration) but rather a desire to know the unknowable. Their quest may be similar to George Leigh Mallory's response to the question, why did he want to climb Mt. Everest? "Because it is there!" Scientists, explorers, adventurers, and pioneers seek to fill in the gaps of human knowledge and understanding.

> "One of man's finest qualities is described by the simple word 'guts'—the ability to take it. If you have the discipline to stand fast when your body wants to run, if you can control your temper and remain cheerful in the face of monotony or disappointment, you have 'guts.'"
> John S. Roosman

Dr. Mihaly Csikszentmihalyi observed that a creative person possesses a high degree of "curiosity, openness, and obsessive perseverance." He states that these characteristics have "to be present to have fresh ideas and then to make them prevail." They also give birth to courage.

Imagine going down an uncharted river filled with plunging rapids, jagged rocks the size of eighteen wheelers, angry brown waters with plumes of spray, and towering cliffs rising sharply from the canyon floor! And imagine making such a dangerous trip having only one arm!

That's what Wes, a geologist, did. On one occasion he and an associate were some 800 feet above the river making scientific observations. They were nearly at a summit, having gained a foothold here and a handhold there in the sheer rock wall. Then Wes found himself unable to pull himself up any further. He could not step back. His muscles trembled. An 80-foot fall yawned before him. Hanging on by his one arm, Wes felt his strength ebbing.

Sweat stung his eyes. If only he had his right arm! He looked up and saw his friend undressing. Surely this wasn't the time or place for a sun bath! Actually, his companion took off his long johns and dangled them down to Wes.

Wes hugged close to the rock wall, released his loosening grip, hung motionless for a terrifying second, and seized the dangling cloth legs. Fortunately the long johns didn't fray or chafe on the sharp rocks above as his friend pulled him to safety.

Once on the ledge above, Wes waited to catch his breath and for his heart to stop racing. Then he calmly walked out on the ledge and completed his scientific observations. He and his friend then returned to their camp beside the river.

Major John Wesley Powell, survivor of the Civil War Battle of Shiloh (where he lost his right arm), was thirty-five when he undertook one of the greatest adventures of all time. He took nine men, four boats, provisions for ten months, and journeyed down the unexplored and uncharted Colorado River in May, 1869. He completed his goal three months later after nine hundred miles of rapids, rocks, and risks.

The day after the cliff mishap, Powell and his fellow explorers set off down the river completely unaware of the dozens of dangerous rapids that lay before them. What are the rapids and rocks that block your journey down the river?

Summary of Key Points

- Scientists, explorers, adventurers, and pioneers seek to fill in the gaps of human knowledge and understanding.
- Curiosity can be a fuel that propels a person to act courageously.
- Creative people possess a high degree of curiosity and tenacity. These attributes are needed to give birth to new ideas. This takes courage.

16

Cornerstone No. 3:

Courage is like a muscle. We can develop it by using it.

The third cornerstone of courage is: **Courage is like a muscle. We can develop it by using it.** Weightlifters build strength by progressively increasing the amount of weight they lift. The same principle applies to cultivating courage. In the case of courage, we are conditioning our body, mind, and spirit for change. Inherent in the process is that we become dissatisfied with the way things are. A comfortable person isn't inclined to change.

> **"The ultimate measure of a man is not where he stands in moments of comfort and convenience, but where he stands at times of challenge and controversy."**
> **Dr. Martin Luther King, Jr.**

While we don't have to practice being miserable, we recognize that building courage, like building strength, requires commitment, discipline, and dedication. We must become intentional about what outcomes we desire to achieve. Personal sacrifices will be necessary.

Imagine how our lives could be transformed if we stepped outside our personal comfort zones! The clever expression, "If we always do what we've always done, we'll always get what we've always gotten," still applies. In addition, comfort zones are really relative positions. They are not only situational depending on the venue—work, home, or various social settings—but they will change in complexity, intensity, and challenge.

Dr. Csikszentmihalyi noted that flow, that is, "being in the zone" or the ontological state of "being" occurs when both skills and challenges pace each other. Nothing remains static. Once a person masters some endeavor, a more demanding challenge must be sought if the person seeks to continue to experience flow. This in turn necessitates more refined or sophisticated skills.

To get a different outcome in our lives means we must do something differently on the front end. The cause and effect relationship tells us that to get a different effect requires a different cause. If we are committed to achieving a new vision, we purposely choose to act in new or different ways.

Summary of Key Points

- Courage is indeed like a muscle. We can develop it by using it.

17

Stepping Outside
Personal Comfort Zones

How do we step outside our four personal comfort zones—physical, intellectual, emotional, spiritual? We do it with courage. There are no shortcuts or fancy psychological formulas.

Most people stumble by attempting to take too great a step at first. When we develop a vision, it is important not to eat more than we can chew. Over-stretched muscles will become damaged and prevent further exercise until they recover. The same applies to stepping too widely outside our comfort zones.

Initially take smaller steps, gain some successes, build some confidence, and then take progressively larger and larger steps. Small increments of personal change will add up over time. Like compound interest, it is the long-term investment instead of the get-rich-quick scheme that we want to pursue.

In Jules Verne's sci-fi thriller, *20,000 Leagues Under the Sea*, the hero, Ned Land, had to step out of his comfort zone and overcome his impatience in order to recover his freedom. Slowly but surely, he was able to do this by taking small steps to change his behavior.

League by league can lead to fatigue.

Mile by mile, you just can't smile.

Yard by yard is hard

But, inch by inch is a cinch.

Step by step is the key!

Maggie was a twenty-four-year-old reporter from Oakland, California. She and another reporter appropriated a jeep and raced to one of Hitler's notorious murder factories called Dachau. The camp was about to be liberated by American troops. As she neared the front gate, the troops remained behind the two reporters. The putrid stench of death hung in the air.

Maggie walked forward. Suddenly the other reporter screamed and pointed. Maggie looked up at the watchtower. There, black-uniformed SS guards, Hitler's most ruthless troopers, had Maggie in the sights of their rifles.

Maggie knew there was no point in running. She'd be cut down before she took a step. She probably wished she could speak into her communicator and say, "Scotty, beam me up!" (But that escape was years into the future.)

Instead she shouted to the Nazi guards, *"Kommen sie hier, bitte!"* And they did! Twenty-two hardcore killers capitulated to a pert blond in khakis. Now, that's one woman you wouldn't want angry at you!

Marguerite Higgins looked fear right in the face and stepped out of her personal comfort zone into a respected reputation of guts. Later during the Korean War, she won the Pulitzer Prize. She was the first woman war correspondent to be so honored. She covered the

Vietnam War for many years and unfortunately died of a rare jungle fever during her 10th trip to that war zone.

Stepping outside our comfort zones doesn't have to be difficult. Small steps still get us to our desired goal. Each small step we take makes us stronger in the corresponding comfort zone.

STEPPING OUTSIDE YOUR PHYSICAL COMFORT ZONE:
(BE SURE TO GET A DOCTOR'S CONCURRENCE, IF NEEDED!)

- If you do not exercise, begin to walk three days a week.

- If you exercise with weights, increase the amount of weights or the number of repetitions you lift.

- If you always take the same route to work, take a different route.

STEPPING OUTSIDE YOUR INTELLECTUAL COMFORT ZONE:

- If you only read two books a year, read one book a quarter.

- If you haven't taken a college course in some time, take a course at the community college or on the internet.

- If you're not a teacher, teach a course, scout group, or discussion group.

STEPPING OUTSIDE YOUR EMOTIONAL COMFORT ZONE:

- If you are an emotionally private person, share your feelings with someone you love.

- If you have a quiet, reserved personality, talk to a newcomer at church, school, or other social gathering.

- If you are an outgoing, talkative person, attempt to speak with another person without using the word "I."

- If you are a forceful, decisive person, withhold your comments until everyone else has spoken.

STEPPING OUTSIDE YOUR SPIRITUAL COMFORT ZONE:

- If you don't have a devotional period during the day, begin one.

- If you've never led a Bible study or Sunday school class, volunteer to lead one.

- If you've never volunteered for a humanitarian or mission trip, join one.

Do you get the idea? Wherever we are, we can do something that we would not normally choose to do. If it makes you somewhat uncomfortable, then you are stretching your courage muscles. Remember, a person who runs the same distance each day no longer stretches his cardiovascular system and thus does not strengthen his body. The idea is to continue to stretch and thereby grow into a person who lives courageously.

Summary of Key Points

- A person can cultivate courage by stepping out of the one's physical, intellectual, emotional, or spiritual comfort zones.
- Step by step is the key. Eat no more than you can chew. This allows self-imposed changes to become mastered and internalized.

18

Ambitious Stretches

Unless we make a conscious effort to grow, we will not be motivated sufficiently to really step out of our comfort zones. Here are five more ambitious stretches that will challenge us:

1. Volunteer in a field or location that is completely new for you.

Dave was an orphan who joined the U.S. Army to get an education. In the Army, soldiers tell you never to volunteer for anything. Dave ignored this advice. He volunteered to work in the mess hall.

Dave worked hard, and the mess sergeant asked Dave if he wanted to go to Cook and Bakers School. He volunteered for the eight-week course. Still later while serving in Germany, Dave volunteered to help his roommate who managed an Enlisted Man's Club (essentially a restaurant operation).

Contrary to conventional wisdom, Dave's volunteering caused him to stretch beyond his current experience. This took courage plus a big dose of hard work, flexibility, and innovation. These same qualities would serve Dave Thomas well when he founded Wendy's International.

2. Mentor someone.

Mentoring helps propagate life skills, values, traditions, and craftsmanship. The relationship that develops between mentor and the person being mentored benefits both parties. Leaders who have a mentor develop at a faster rate and avoid having to rediscover the wheel as many times.

3. Forgive someone (perhaps even face-to-face).

Forgiveness is something we do for ourselves not for the person who hurt us. Forgiveness does not mean forgetting what happened or granting the other party a free pass for whatever we think they did. Rather, it is a clearing or cleansing of the emotional grip it has upon us so we can get on with our lives.

Gandhi once noted that darkness in one area of our lives tends to pollute or negatively influence all other aspects of our lives. Such is the case where we harbor a grudge, bitterness, anger, or hatred of another person. If allowed to fester, such a canker will corrode your spirit and control your mind.

4. Actually listen to someone.

Listening is a critical people skill! It is both a sign of respect and an effective way to build trust. Although people use their ears more than any other communications tool, including speaking, reading, or writing, few people ever receive any formal training in school about effective listening. And for many, listening is a stretch outside a comfort zone.

There are three secrets of effective listening. The first is to listen with your eyes. The main sensors we want to bring to bear are our ears. Fortunately, our ears are bore-sighted with our eyes. Wherever our eyes go, our ears will follow. We need to be looking at the person speaking.

For example, in a crowded room, my eyes need to be focused on the person who's speaking. If my eyes drift away to look at another person in the room, what do you think my first words will be when I look back at him? "What did you say?" Once one's eyes wander from the person speaking, one's ears are no longer optimized for listening.

This brings up an important point. One reason we need to focus and stay alert to the speaker involves the speed at which we can listen. Most people speak between 100 and 250 words a minute. On the other hand, our minds can think at 600-900 words a minute. If someone were speaking at 100 words a minute, and we listen at 600 words a minute, we have some left over capacity to think about something else. If we do that, we're not really listening!

In addition, listening with our eyes allows us to see the nonverbal language that the speaker is showing. Body language may give you some important clues as to what the speaker is really saying. Most people are adept enough to disguise their words. For example, if you ask someone, "How are you doing?" they typically will say, "I'm fine." The person may or may not be truthful. Most people, however, are unable to mask their body language. A frowning face or body contorted with worry would immediately tell you they're not fine. So once again, we listen with our eyes.

The second secret of effective listening is to see with your heart. This is what I call generous listening. This means we listen to another person as if what's about to come out of his mouth is golden. Imagine if someone you esteemed a great deal were speaking, like the former Secretary of State, Colin Powell, or filmmaker Steven Spielberg. You'd be all ears! You'd hover over every word hoping to get a nugget or two that would help you in some way. You can use the very same approach with everyone you meet. Perhaps they have the missing clue you need to solve one of your greatest challenges.

The third secret of effective listening is to listen from three points of view: first, the content of the words; second, the emotion behind the words; and third, the context of the words. The content of the words encompasses the facts that are spoken or the information that is given. This is the level on which we usually listen. The emotion behind the words tells us whether the speaker is joyful, sad, frustrated, disappointed, fearful, and the like. The context of the words refers to the background or situation on which the underlying conversation is based. Generous listening can be considered a context where the listener seeks to understand everything that is being communicated.

So all you need to do is listen. It's simple, isn't it? It's simple, but not easy! Effective listening takes discipline!

You must listen on purpose. Listening is not merely waiting for your turn to speak. More important, nothing that comes out of your mouth will teach you anything new. You only learn new ideas by listening intently to someone else. So, listen with your eyes, see with your heart, and be conscious of the content, emotions, and context of the speaker's words!

> ## "The courage to speak must be matched by the wisdom to listen."
> **Anonymous**

5. Be flexible and suspend your point of view.

As people grow older, they tend to become more intolerant of other people's opinions. Unfortunately some people possess a righteousness about them from an early age. If you want to stifle a child's curiosity or self-esteem, simply insist on being right, or winning every game of checkers. What about dealing with adults? Being right means the other person is wrong. Most issues and opinions in life are not that absolute or clear cut.

For the sake of organizational unity and cohesiveness, it makes more sense to be flexible by suspending your point of view when the situation is not critical. Let the more junior members express their thoughts as a way of getting them to participate.

Stepping out of our comfort zones may not be pleasurable, but it is essential if we hope to cultivate courage. If we are ever going to achieve our vision, we must take that first step. Remember Charles Atlas and his railroad car feat? Once the train begins to move, it will take less work to keep it in motion.

Overcoming our mental inertia becomes the critical step in our methodology. What does it take to overcome it? It takes courage. How do we develop courage? We do it by routinely stepping outside our behavioral comfort zones.

Summary of Key Points

- Volunteering, mentoring, forgiving, and being flexible challenge our basic nature.
- Listen with your eyes, see with your heart, and listen to the speaker's words for content, emotion, and context.
- Listening is an active sport, not a passive one. One must listen on purpose.
- To be right means that someone must be wrong. Become more flexible, and suspend your point of view where appropriate.

19

Making Change
a Challenge Not a Curse

We condition our bodies, our minds, and our spirits to experience change. If we are to dream big dreams and make them a reality, we should be prepared to do something that we are currently not doing.

We may be aware of the boundaries of our comfort zones but often have a blind spot identifying them. Or we know what will stretch us, but due to fear, we choose not to expose ourselves to change.

Change is inevitable in our lives. When we orchestrate the change, we feel more comfortable with it. After all, who likes surprises? Surprisingly, we all do! Think about birthday presents or Christmas gifts. The unknown may make other surprises less welcome, but how do we know these other surprises will not be as enjoyable and as full of potential as our birthday presents?

We need a way to condition our minds to change. If we can become more acclimatized to change, our fear of it will diminish! So we need to practice raising the bar and stretching out of our personal comfort zones.

There are some additional ways that will help us develop our courage muscles. This brings us to the One Plus Technique™.

One Pl s Techniq e™

1. If you can take one step, you can take one more.

2. If you can hold on for one minute, you can hold on for one more.

3. If you can make one beneficial suggestion, you can make one more.

4. Don't stop and stay where you are. Always take one more step.

5. Everyone can take small steps. Giant leaps aren't necessary.

6. Small steps can still get us to our desired goal. There is really nothing to fear. We think we are taking a big risk, but in reality it's only a small one!

> **"Co rage is fear**
> **holding on a min te longer."**
> **General George S. Patton, Jr., U.S. Army**

Changing Your Perspective

Another approach that will help a person strengthen his or her courage muscles is the ability to change one's perspective. Stretching one's thinking will change one's actions and help a person become more resilient in the face of changing circumstances. A daily recommitment to the new perspective will lock it into your way of life.

- Adopt an optimistic view of the future versus a negative view.
- Commit yourself to proactivity instead of procrastination.
- Embrace excellence instead of perfection.
- Accept being at risk instead of playing it safe.
- Be real with others instead of playing roles and wearing false masks.
- Commit to taking a stand instead of making an exit.
- Get personally involved instead of remaining uncommitted.
- Be a victor not a victim.

> **"Courage is not the towering oak that sees storms come and go; it is the fragile blossom that opens in the snow."**
> Alice M. Swaim

Surviving a Calamity

Life is full of surprises, some pleasant and some extremely painful. After suffering a defeat or setback, courageous people pick themselves off the ground and move forward again. Surviving a calamity is a combination of good fortune and mental attitude. Virgil, the classical Roman poet, noted, "Every calamity is to be overcome by endurance." Here are some observations my wife and I gleaned from Hurricane Katrina:

- Be thankful for what you have and count your blessings since you are alive!
- It's normal to despair and feel depressed. Post traumatic stress symptoms don't obey any calendar.
- What you had before in terms of people, places, and relationships will never be the same again, but you will make new relationships and memories.
- Continue to look forward and move forward.
- Focus on what you have and not what you have lost.
- Get a clearer picture of what is important— relationships and experiences with family and friends, not possessions.
- Continue to be productive and engaged in life.

> **"Courage doesn't always roar. Sometimes courage is the little voice at the end of the day that says I'll try again tomorrow."**
> **Mary Anne Radmacher**

Making Change Your Ally

Most of us would prefer to duck change. Just when we think we are on an even keel and can sit back to enjoy the ride, some rogue wave upsets our equilibrium. Such is real life!

Change can also be a source of stress in our lives. How does stress make you feel? Fearful? Uncomfortable? Excited? Anxious? Uncertain? We all have different reactions to stress based on circumstances. Some stress keeps us alert and on our toes. This has a positive effect on performance. Negative stress, however, can work at cross purposes with being courageous.

Changes seem to be coming at us faster than ever before. When asked what was the difference between his 1962 Mercury capsule spaceflight and his 1998 Space Shuttle flight, John Glenn said, "I drank orange-flavored Tang on the first trip into space and orange-flavored Metamucil on the next trip." Of course, the technology between the two courageous events was miles apart!

We have terrorism and rap music. We have genetic engineering and nanotechnology. We have extremely sophisticated cell phones with GPS. Over time we tend to grow accustomed to changes, and they cease to have the impact they did when they first materialized. Some changes, like terrorism, create ongoing stress. Are you as worried about terrorism now as you were on September 10th?

Winston Churchill believed, "There is nothing wrong with change if it is in the right direction. To improve is to change; to be perfect is to change often." We all like some change, like getting a new car. Unplanned changes, however, may make us uncomfortable.

If you collected vinyl records or had stock in a company that made carburetors, then you were not terribly excited with having to buy CDs of your favorite music or watch your stock decrease in value due to fuel injectors.

How do you feel about a square hamburger? I tend to prefer round ones. Three of my kids worked at Wendy's while they were in high school. One of my sons was the grill man. On one particularly busy night, they ran out of square meat. My son was outraged at having to borrow some "circle meat" from another fast food restaurant down the street. (The reason why Wendy's has square burgers: At Wendy's they don't cut corners!)

> ## "One man with courage makes a majority."
> ### Andrew Jackson

Winston Churchill also observed that, "A change is as good as a rest." In his charming little book, *Painting as a Pastime*, he talked about the impact of change on a busy person. He maintained that if you spend the day doing paperwork, then reading may not give your brain its needed rest.

Churchill discovered the joy of painting after being forced from office as the First Lord of the Admiralty following the Dardanelles and Gallipoli fiascos. Churchill was the scapegoat for a brilliant strategic plan to undo the stalemate on the Western Front.

The idea is to balance stressful activities with ones that give you some relief. Isn't that what we call fun? Churchill also had some good wisdom as to what you should do either as a profession or as a hobby. He said, "Do what you like, but like what you do."

Using Churchill's approach, here are some suggested leisure activities that balance job stresses:

Using Change to Reduce Workplace Stress

If your job requires	Consider an activity like
Much sitting or mental concentration	Aerobic exercise
Mindless repetition	Mentally challenging activities
A controlled environment	Hiking in nature, adventure
Boring tasks or no recognition	Competitive activities
Responding to people's demands	Solitary activities
Dealing with conflict	Peaceful activities
Working alone	Social activities

Speaking of balance, we recognize that with each of life's endeavors come certain consequences or responsibilities. Gandhi observed that life balance means avoiding:

- Wealth without work
- Pleasure without conscience
- Knowledge without character
- Commerce without morality
- Science without humanity
- Religion without sacrifice
- Politics without principle

If we seek to become more courageous men and women, we need to use change to make us stronger and more resilient. And by fortifying ourselves by cultivating courage, we discover that courage is a catalyst for change. Thus, it takes change to build our courage and our courage can also produce change. We can make change work for us.

"God grant me the courage not to give up what I think is right, even though I think it is hopeless."
Fleet Admiral Chester W. Nimitz, U.S. Navy

Summary of Key Points

- The One Plus Technique™ enables us to take small steps that do not present a big risk.
- We can cultivate courage by changing our perspectives.
- We can always choose how we react to circumstances. Choose an empowering perspective instead of a discouraging one.
- Surviving a calamity means focusing on what you have, not what you have lost. Continue to look forward/move forward.
- Leaders find ways to make change and stress work for them.
- Courage is a catalyst for change.

20

Benchmarking Heroes and Role Models

Nothing gives us a better picture of courageous behavior than the real-life examples of other people. But what does a hero look like? All too often we are influenced by what we see on television or in the movies. In America, movie stars make up the top percentage of people born with good looks. Rarely is a Hollywood star anything but elegant and good looking. We tend to envision our male heroes as tall, dark, and handsome or perhaps tall, strong, and blond.

> ## "My hero is Man the Discoverer."
> ### Dr. Daniel J. Boorstin

Real life has a different model for heroes. Some are short, overweight, and bald—like Winston Churchill; or tall, gaunt, and ungainly—like Lincoln; or short, skinny, and aloof—like T. E. Lawrence (of Arabia); or quiet, unassuming, and emaciated—like Gandhi. What about

Golda Meir, Harry Truman, or George Patton? They didn't look like movie stars, did they?

We also need to make a distinction between a hero and a celebrity. The former is someone admired for his or her achievements, noble qualities, and bravery. The latter is someone who is popular and famous. A hero may be a celebrity, but a celebrity isn't necessarily a hero.

Historian Paul Johnson ascribes four characteristics to recognize heroes today. First, they think independently and "treat what is the current consensus with skepticism." Second, they act "resolutely and consistently." Third, they remain committed to their endeavor regardless of what others say. Fourth, they "act with personal courage at all times, regardless of the consequences" to themselves. Johnson then puts an exclamation mark on this last element. "All history teaches that there is no substitute for courage. It is the noblest and best of all qualities, and the one indispensable element in heroism in all its different manifestations."

> **"My heroes tend to be people who successfully accomplish things I would not dare even to contemplate."**
> **Paul Johnson**

When I was twelve, I began reading biographies and autobiographies about Generals MacArthur, Patton, Eisenhower, and Bradley. In later years, I added T. E. Lawrence, John Buchan, Ayn Rand, Admiral Arleigh Burke, Camille Pissarro, Hugo Eckener, and Admiral

Charles Rosendahl. One individual I "discovered" while I was in 10th grade would change my life forever.

On Sunday, January 24, 1965, I was sitting in my father's chair in our suburban Los Angeles home reading the *L. A. Times* and listening to the radio. The 1:00 PM news opened with the announcement of the death of Sir Winston Churchill. As I listened to the news story, I experienced a sense of sadness. This confused me since I did not really know much about him. A question formed in my mind: "Who was Winston Churchill?"

As I soon discovered, Churchill lived a long life, and my interest in him occupied me a great deal longer than I ever expected.

My curiosity about Churchill followed me as I served as a career naval officer, private school administrator, professional speaker, and seminar leader. I published articles and a book about Churchill, took up oil painting largely because of his example, gave hundreds of speeches and presentations about him nationwide, served a term on the Board of Directors of the International Churchill Society, and met (and later married) the woman of my dreams at a Churchill Society convention.

January 24, 1965, may have been Sir Winston's final hour, but for me it was the birth of a life-long study of Churchill and of ways to share his leadership wisdom to help others attain their finest hour.

Winston Churchill's example of courage was impressive and well documented. There are some two thousand books about Churchill and roughly twenty new titles emerge every year. Some of Churchill's courageous actions include:

- As a journalist during the Cuban insurrection against Spain in 1885, he observed hostilities.
- As army officer fighting hostile tribesmen in Afghanistan in 1897, he distinguished himself while under fire.
- As a cavalry officer in the Battle of Omdurman in the Sudan in 1898, he took part in the last great cavalry charge.
- As a war correspondent during the Boer War 1899-1900, he played a heroic role in the defense and escape of an armored train.
- As a POW, he successfully escaped from the Boers in 1899 traveling over 300 miles to safety.
- As an army officer during the Boer War, 1899-1900, he took part in the Battle of Spion Kop and bicycled through Johannesburg to convey dispatches and intelligence to separated British forces.
- Learned to fly in 1913 when airplanes were primitive inventions.
- As a battalion commander in the trenches on the Western Front in 1915, he made numerous forays into no-man's land to gather intelligence.
- As First Lord of the Admiralty, he flew to France numerous times to persuade the French not to surrender in 1940.
- As Prime Minister during World War II exposed himself to danger during the German air attacks during the Blitz, 1940-1941.
- As Prime Minister, he flew long range missions numerous times, often through contested air space, to visit FDR and Stalin.

Churchill's many acts of physical courage were matched by his moral courage:

- Crossed the floor (changed political party) in Parliament in 1904 and 1924.
- Instituted minimum wage (1909), prison reform (1910), and widows' pensions (1914)
- Gave wings to the Royal Naval Air Service in 1911.
- Converted the Royal Navy from coal to oil in 1914.
- Coordinated the defense of beleaguered Antwerp in 1914.
- Fostered the development of the tank in 1915.
- Proposed a brilliant Dardanelles strategy to counter the Western Front stalemate in 1915.
- Embraced a total quality leadership approach for the Ministry of Munitions in 1917.
- Supported the Zionist movement 1920.
- Reorganized boundaries in the Middle East in 1921.
- Warned of the gathering storm posed by Hitler and Nazi Germany 1932-1939.
- Refused to negotiate with Hitler in 1940 as members of the British War Cabinet debated the issue.
- Spoke resolutely and defiantly when Britain stood alone in 1940-1941.
- Prophesized the coming of the Cold War in 1946.

We can learn to model heroic behavior by studying the lives of genuine heroes. I strongly suggest books or documentaries instead of Hollywood movies. Even in the best movies, the historical truth and context are often sacrificed for the story line or love interest. Developing a historical perspective can be invaluable when daunting, real-life events occur. (See Appendix D: Suggested Books about Courage and Appendix E: Suggested Movies about Courage.)

Concerning heroes and role models, we have another choice to consider. We can either be intimidated by their examples or we can be inspired to emulate their behavior. Who are your heroes? How have they influenced your life?

> "Stories of the past offer hope and inspiration, but they cannot supply courage itself. For this, each person must look into his own soul."
> John F. Kennedy

Summary of Key Points

- Heroes act with personal courage regardless of the consequences to themselves.
- Heroes and role models can be a great source of inspiration.
- When considering heroes, use their varied achievements as a source of inspiration, not intimidation.

21

More Courage Muscle Flexing

Patience

Courageous people are rarely impulsive. They gather the facts and take appropriate action. Using the proverbial "don't shoot until you see the whites of their eyes," the courageous person is patient while the less courageous seemingly reacts without adequate deliberation.

Cultivating patience requires patience. In Japan, young children are taught origami, paper folding, to help them develop patience. In our modern, fast-paced world, we find it difficult to wait for anything.

Our infatuation with speed (whether boiling water in the microwave or connecting on the internet) has conditioned us for action and activity. Today it's almost impossible to sit still and watch an outstanding (albeit black and white) leadership movie like *Twelve O'clock High* and not feel bored by its glacial pace.

Unfortunately we cannot accelerate that which moves at a fixed rate. We can't grow a giant sequoia according to our schedule. Nor can we can develop wisdom quickly. Building a team is no different. It takes time to build relationships and develop trust.

- Successful people tend to be patient, uncomplaining, and cheerful
- Leaders are patiently open minded as they interact with other people
- "Be quick to listen, slow to speak, slow to become angry"
- Courageous leaders create an environment that encourages discussion
- We want our teams to think from as many different perspectives as possible
- Problem solvers must generate as many options and potential solutions as possible for the decision makers

Creativity

We can also flex and strengthen our courage muscles by being creative yet pragmatic. Instead of having our workers bring their problems for us to solve, why not empower them? Ask them for three different ways to solve a problem and recommendation which would be best for the given situation. Give ownership by asking people what they think instead of asking them to check their brains at the front door when they arrive at work in the morning.

Being courageous means looking at a problem from different points of view. Brainstorming in a light-hearted, casual environment seems to work best.

Creativity cannot be legislated to occur on demand like ordering a cup of coffee!

Since most of the businesses within a given industry solve problems in much the same way, looking outside that industry may give some valuable ways to find new, if not unique, solutions. For example, perhaps a travel agency is looking for a way to deal with a new challenge. They might consider how several different industries would address the problem from their point of view— medical, food service, accounting, newspaper. The key is to benchmark best practices from other industries or fields and apply them to your problems. It takes courage to attempt something new.

Get Physically Stronger

Physical strength builds confidence and resilience. When we are in good physical condition, we are also able to deal with stressful challenges better. I'm not suggesting that Charles Atlas had more courage than Gandhi. Rather, a physically fit person will have more reserves to deal with challenges and problems. They might give a person an edge in being more courageous when the moment arises.

A physically fit person can deal with adversity and physical hardships better, too. In January, 2005, I started an intensive weight-lifting exercise regime. (I have pushed weights on and off since I rowed on UCLA's men's crew in the late 1960s. There were years, however, when I did little recreational workouts due to jobs that left me with little spare time or energy.) For three days a week I worked out for an hour. I wondered to myself why I was so motivated to do this. In less than a year I found out.

On Friday, August 26th, my wife and I were in Durham, NC, for a large family reunion to celebrate the 90th birthday of my mother-in-law. When Hurricane Katrina's track shifted from the Florida panhandle to the Louisiana/ Mississippi border, I knew we had to get home right away. My wife and I reluctantly departed early Saturday morning and drove 729 miles back to Pascagoula.

The next morning, Sunday, I started putting up metal hurricane shutters and plywood on my home and office. As is typically the case before a hurricane strikes, it was a terribly hot, uncomfortably humid day. The weather, fatigue, and apprehension sapped my strength. Had I not previously conditioned my body to hardship, I might not have been able to respond adequately.

Since we never know when we will be called upon to react with a Herculean effort, we need to prepare our bodies and minds in less demanding periods.

Do you get regular exercise? If you're not exercising your muscles and heart on the job, then you're going to need to begin exercising. Exercise can also help you deal with stress, frustrations, and anger. But before you begin an exercise routine, I hope you'll exercise caution! Visit a doctor before any new program. Play it safe.

There are three general categories for exercising:

- Aerobic exercise, with 3-5 days a week of 25-45 minutes duration where you exercise at 60%-70% of your maximum heart rate.

- Stretching exercises, where you stretch before and after aerobics with 30 seconds to 2 minutes per stretch. Remember, don't bounce or you may tear muscles.

- Toning exercises, with weights or the equivalent resistance. To build strength, use higher resistance with lower repetitions. To build endurance, use lower resistance with more reps.

There are many activities you can do that will help you get stronger physically. Do the ones you enjoy most—aerobics, walking, jogging, weightlifting, Tai chi, bicycling, swimming, martial arts, hiking, playing team sports, and the like. Ropes courses also offer an opportunity to develop your courage.

During my four years rowing on UCLA's crew, I discovered first-hand that the mind will quit before the body does. We rowed almost 3,000 miles every year. A typical "round trip" inside Marina del Rey was four miles, and we often raced our three or four boats during our daily workouts. There were ample opportunities to row with when the gas tank was on empty. A sign in our locker room proclaimed, "Conditioning is physical. Toughness is a state of mind. One without the other is a mockery!"

> **"Fatigue makes cowards of us all."**
> **General George S. Patton, Jr., U.S. Army**

So getting stronger physically really means getting mentally tougher. By stretching our physical activity using the One Plus Technique™, we can improve our physical as well as our mental performance and hence our confidence, self-esteem, and courage.

The service academies at Annapolis, West Point, and Colorado Springs have known for years that team sports can prepare people for real-life trials in later life. Team sports can be a valuable source of camaraderie, teamwork, and discipline infused with a balanced risk-reduction quality. When properly used, team sports can help individuals and teams to become more courageous.

I remember coaching youth soccer and the impact team sports had on a group of rowdy twelve-year-olds. The better athletes all wanted to play forward so they could be in a position to score. I was more interested in developing the team both offensively and defensively. Team play was more important than individual achievement.

During one game, I placed one of the boys, Josh, who typically played as a defender, as one of my three forwards. At a critical part of the game, he kicked a goal. The look on that boy's face was priceless! For the rest of the game and during subsequent games in the season, he played with more confidence and energy.

Josh's goal also helped the team coalesce better. Several of the less athletic players realized that perhaps they, too, might be able to score. Their contributions on the playing field increased dramatically!

> **"On these fields of friendly strife are sown the seeds that on other fields and other days will bear the fruits of victory."**
> **General Douglas MacArthur, U.S. Army**

I think we all react positively to a success. Small successes over time help build self-esteem. Being part of a team sport helps us harness the power of the team to achieve success. Each team member can benefit from the achievements of the team as a whole.

Remembering Past Successes

Sometimes recalling past successes can be a way to prepare ourselves for future challenges. Keeping a victory log might be a means of documenting successes. Consulting this before an upcoming trial or challenging moment may give us strength and confidence that we have overcome difficult situations in the past and can do so again.

Summary of Key Points

- Courageous people exercise patience.
- We can use best practices from other industries to solve problems and thus strengthen our courage muscles.
- Getting stronger physically can give us greater confidence.
- "Fatigue makes cowards of us all."
- A victory log can help us prepare for future challenges by remembering past successes.

22

Cornerstone No. 4:

Courage resides in everyone.

There is untapped potential that exists in every person in our organizations. Every person, I repeat, every person, has the capacity for leadership. Every person has the capacity for creativity. And most important, *every* person has the capacity for courage! The fourth cornerstone of courage captures this equalitarian quality of courage: **Courage resides in everyone.**

Unfortunately, we rarely utilize this incredible resource of talent. Failure to use this costs our organizations billions of dollars in lost revenue not to mention losing the hearts and minds of capable people.

In conversations with tellers, administrative assistants, lab technicians, librarians, and others further down in the corporate feeding chain, I discovered natural leaders who were unaware of their strengths. Since they were not occupying a leadership position in their organization, they did not consider themselves a leader.

Organizations who embrace quality recognize more than most that leadership and creativity among more junior workers are essential for business success. Process action, process improvement, and Six Sigma project teams that listen to the voices of those who actually do the work find better ways to streamline processes and make them more productive.

And while the potential for courage resides in every person, no one can predict how any person will react in a crisis. We generally assume that the more senior, better-trained individuals will exhibit more courage. Training, as noted earlier, does prepare a person to confront new situations better. Often times, a more junior person is called upon to respond to a crisis before the better-trained personnel arrive.

> "Courage is a quality you grow into, like filling bigger shoes. The more you walk in them, the more comfortable they get."
> **Retired UK Police Inspector David J. Farley**

Summary of Key Points

- Courage resides in everyone.
- Everyone has the capacity to be a leader, to be creative, and to exercise courage.
- Organizations often fail to tap into the talents, creativity, and energy of every worker.
- No one can predict who will be courageous during a crisis.

23

Building Boldness

Courage sits dormant in each of us. Just as we can condition our courage muscles to potentially respond to some demand, we can also stimulate our ability to respond courageously. Here are some ways to do this:

1. Compete in challenging situations by taking difficult assignments.

In Anton Myrer's 1976 novel, *Once an Eagle*, we read about two Army officers whose careers spanned the end of World War I until the early phases of the war in Vietnam. The two contrasting characters were Sam Damon (played by Sam Elliot in the television movie) and Courtney Massengale (played by Cliff Potts). Massengale was a politician and sycophant. He was obsessed with career advancement regardless of the cost to others. He took the easy way out and hoped to advance in the Army due to political influence. Damon, on the other hand, was a professional soldier, a true warrior, committed to his men and the mission. He took the tough assignments and often suffered injustices because of his honesty, integrity, and loyalty. Can you imagine who was the more courageous of the two officers?

> **"It is not because things are difficult that we dare not venture. It is because we dare not venture that they are difficult."**
> **Lucius Annaeus Seneca**

Although I was a Surface Warfare Officer in the Navy, what we called being a "ship driver," I was by shipboard experience and postgraduate education a weapons subspecialist. I knew about employing and maintaining naval guns, guided missiles, associated fire control radars, torpedoes, small arms, and the like. I had a basic understanding of the ship's engineering plant but really had no interest in ever being a "snipe" in the engineering department.

After completing a tour as Weapons Officer in the fleet frigate, *USS Brewton (FF 1086),* I desired to remain in Pearl Harbor, Hawaii, for my second department head tour. My detailer granted my wish but assigned me to the guided missile cruiser, *USS Worden (CG 18)* as Engineer Officer.

Being chief engineer in a twenty-year-old steam plant like *Worden* was one of the most challenging tours in the surface navy in those days. The waterfront was littered with chief engineers, and even some commanding officers, who were relieved for cause over failure to meet certain engineering standards.

It was an exceptionally difficult tour leading and managing an engineering department of over 100 officers and men as they maintained two fire rooms and two engine rooms, each containing over 2000 valves, scores of steam and electric pumps, and miles of steam, fuel, water, and air piping. Our four 1200-psi 950°F superheated boilers and main engines were the heart of the plant. A great deal of other steam, electric, hydraulic, and pneumatic equipment provided for the ship's mobility, power, and water to support all combat systems and hotel necessities of the warship. Eighty-hour or longer work weeks were not uncommon when the ship was in port and were longer still when we were at sea.

Surprisingly, I thoroughly enjoyed my tour as Engineer. The challenges were the most demanding I ever experienced, but I learned and grew the most. My officers and men achieved great successes, and I was proud to be permitted to lead them.

> ## "Freedom lies in being bold."
> ### Robert Frost

Do not duck the challenging, high-risk positions! You will benefit greatly from the experience, and your new confidence will help you tackle future tests.

2. Broaden your experience.

The familiar is like eating comfort food. It calms and soothes us. Unfortunately, it does not prepare us for greater challenges and demands. Who do you think would be a better leader of an organization—someone who spent an entire career in one department or someone who served in many areas? We can learn more about ourselves and can serve our organizations better if we have both depth and breadth of experience.

Just as I benefited from a tour in the engineering department, you will be more valuable to your organization and yourself if you deliberately seek wide, diversified experience in your career field. Dr. Richard W. Hamming believed, "Voyeurism is no substitute for experience."

3. Develop sound judgment.

We develop sound judgment by attempting to do things that are challenging even if we might make mistakes. We can adopt a discerning attitude to everything we see, do, and learn. Leaders ask two crucial questions:

- **So what?** That is, what is significant about this?

- **Now what?** What will you do differently? What specific, measurable actions will you take today? And why?

Our ability to do the right thing at the right time comes from not doing the right things at the right times and learning from our errors. It may be painful, but it is a powerful way to ultimately be more successful.

Developing judgment doesn't just come from experience but also from study. Enhancing our knowledge of the issues and challenges gives us a deeper foundation to support what we can do action wise.

> **"If you want to increase your success, double your failure rate."**
> **Thomas J. Watson, Sr.**

4. Critique your individual and team battles, tasks, and training.

After-action critiques are critical! They help us improve everything we do. We can eliminate steps that:

- Do not contribute to the desired outcomes.
- Are redundant.
- Do not add value to the customer.
- Are not user friendly.

Our critiques need to address:

- What went right?
- What went wrong?
- What can be done differently next time?

Fundamental in all after-action critiques are implementing the new desired changes. I have known organizations that kept logs of corrective actions they hoped to incorporate but never did. They made the same mistakes repeatedly. Not surprisingly, some of these organizations no longer exist.

Critiques are at the core of the continuous improvement attitude. The Plan-Do-Check-Act methodology of statistical process control was originally proposed by Walter A. Shewhart and was promoted by Deming. Checking one's performance and applying corrective actions are the key to enhancing future performance.

Refining our actions to be more effective at what we do becomes an attitude not just an activity. It is the iterative nature of this process that accrues more positive results over time. And we must allow sufficient time to master and internalize process and behavior changes. As Ed Deming would say, "There's no instant pudding!"

Plan

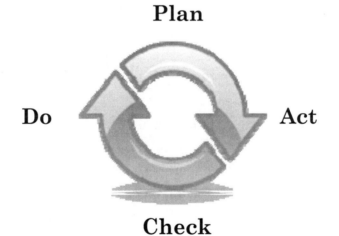

Do **Act**

Check

Continuous improvement seeks to streamline the processes of any evolution as well as build some accountability into them. Do you really follow your stated policies and processes? If not, either enforce them or change them to reflect what you actually want done.

Open, honest communications are encouraged. That means: no spin, no complaining, no gossiping, and no finger pointing! As noted earlier, it's important to celebrate courageous acts publicly. This reaffirms and reinforces values of your workplace or home. And it gives people positive role models to emulate.

Summary of Key Points

- Build boldness by accepting difficult assignments as well as by broadening one's experiences.
- Develop sound judgment by adopting a discerning attitude. Ask the questions "so what?" and "now what?" at every opportunity.
- Critique individual and team battles with the plan-do-check-act method.

24

Decisiveness

Courageous people are decisive. John Maxwell made an interesting observation regarding decision making and success. He noted:

Decision versus Consequence

Wrong decision at the wrong time = **DISASTER**
Wrong decision at the right time = Mistake
Right decision at the wrong time = Rejection
Right decision at the right time = **SUCCESS!!!**

We may not know beforehand whether our decisions are right or wrong or whether they came at the appropriate time. But we need the courage to respond based on the best information we have available. Do what needs to be done, and let history, not the timid, pass judgment.

To go or not to go, that was the decision. It was June 4th, 1944. The buffeting wind caused the rain to travel horizontally. General Eisenhower wasn't really sure what the weather would be on June 6th. The Allied invasion of Europe had already been postponed one day due to bad weather. Over a million soldiers in Southern England would eventually be spotted by German spies or patrolling aircraft. A vast logistic train of supplies was loaded and ready to proceed to France. Ike had to decide.

A decision to invade might cost the lives of 30,000 men. A decision to postpone the invasion again could cost even more men in the long run and might change the outcome of the war. General Eisenhower chose to attack. His decision took courage!

My time in destroyers taught me a methodology to reach decisions. The first part of the process involved determining what the problem was. All too often, we fail to solve the real problem. Once the actual problem is identified, then it is vital to understand the nature of the problem—the variables, constraints, and guidance, if any, from higher authority. Then decision makers identify various ways to solve the problem, assess the worst-case solution, best-case solution, most likely outcome, easiest solution to carry out, and impact of the solution on other related problems. Finally, given the inputs from the preceding analysis, a best solution is selected and implemented.

The whole decision process may need to be compressed when enemy gunfire is falling about your ship. In that case, rapid, accurate response is critical. Under more relaxed circumstances, a more thorough investigation of the various possibilities can be explored. The mission, however, remains to take some appropriate action in a timely manner. Endlessly debating a problem or forming study groups, unfortunately, never takes the place of decisive action.

DESTROYERMEN'S APPROACH™
to Decision Making

1. What is the problem?
2. What are various options to solve the problem?
3. What is the worst-case solution?
4. What is the best-case, highest-payoff solution?
5. What is the most likely outcome for each solution?
6. Are there any force multipliers in a solution?
7. What is the most easily-executed solution?
8. Based on the above, what is the best solution to the problem?

Summary of Key Points

- Decision making requires courage.
- The Destroyermen's Approach gives a method for selecting the best solution.

25

DISC and Decision Making

In my books, *The Churchill Factors: Creating Your Finest Hour* and *The Greatest Board in the World*, I describe people as having a combination of four behavioral characteristics. These descriptions are derived from the Inscape Publishing DISC Dimensions of Behavior model. For each of us, one or two of these characteristics tends to be predominant.

DISC Behavioral Traits

- **Drivers:** bottom line, mission oriented, direct, fast paced.

- **Influencers:** people oriented, outgoing, verbal, lighthearted, fast paced.

- **Supporters:** warm, relational, meticulous, quiet, reserved pace.

- **Conceptualizers:** high standards of accuracy and quality independent, detail oriented, reserved pace.

Depending on a person's behavioral style, there is a variance in the way decisions are made. Drivers reach their decision fastest and attempt to create a framework for generating potential solutions. Unfortunately they tend not to share with others how they got from point A to point B. Influencers tend to avoid details and are often susceptible to emotions and other people's opinions. Supporters will involve others in the decision process. Conceptualizers often have difficulties reaching a decision since they put it off until they have complete information. In the real world, decision makers rarely have all the information that they really want. Yet, they must still make a decision.

> **"The world is not perishing for the want of clever or talented or well-meaning men. It is perishing for the want of men of courage and resolution."**
> **Robert J. McCracken**

DISC Decision Making

- **Drivers**: Quick, reactive, results-focused, may lack sufficient information.

- **Influencers**: Spontaneous, emotional, gut feel, swayed by opinion, not detail oriented

- **Supporters**: Trusting, generous acceptance, methodical, in collaboration with others, intuitive.

- **Conceptualizers**: Need more info and time, diplomatic, unable to decide.

Decision making is one way we adapt to change. Each of the four different behavioral styles has a different tendency with respect to change. In general, Drivers are most tolerant of change. They tend to be change setters. At the other extreme are Supporters who are uncomfortable with change, especially rapid change. This implies that Supporters will need to be more courageous in their actions when dealing with change than drivers will need to be. While this may not always be the case, Supporters typically need to become comfortable with smaller bite-sized pieces of change.

> **"A pearl is the outcome
> of a problem well managed."**
> **Dr. Paul L. Escamilla**

Adaptability to Change
Exhibited by Different DISC Styles

- **Drivers**: Will embrace change if they do not lose control of the situation.

- **Influencers**: Will embrace change if they are involved in it with other people.

- **Supporters**: Will embrace change if they are gradually conditioned to the change. Supporters do not like rapid change.

- **Conceptualizers**: Will embrace change if they have enough information to justify the change.

Awareness of a person's dominant DISC characteristics is valuable since it tells leaders how to work best with people of different styles. One size does not fit all! Knowing whether someone is an impulsive decision maker (Influencer) or needs to be conditioned to accept change (Supporter) enables us to interact best with those kinds of people.

Summary of Key Points

- Leaders understand how the four different behavioral styles reach a decision and adapt to change. This gives them valuable information about their people and their capabilities.

26

Cornerstone No. 5:

Courage is contagious.

Imagine you're sitting in a large audience at a leadership conference. The conference speaker asks you to stand up by yourself. How do you think you'd feel? A little nervous, self-conscious, and perhaps intimidated? Then the conference speaker asks the people on each side of you to stand up. Does that feel a little better? Finally, the speaker asks the entire audience to stand. That feels great! There is a contagious sigh of relief when everyone is asked to stand up.

What else is contagious? How about colds, optimism, negativism, anger, enthusiasm, pride, laughter, fear, and courage? The fifth cornerstone of courage is: **Courage is contagious.** Courage, like fear, seems to have a transmittable quality to it. A number of courageous people in a group can cause others in the group to be courageous. As Dr. Escamilla accurately observed, "Courage finds its clearest voice in the company of others."

Isn't it normal for men in combat to experience fear, especially first-timers to war? Fear follows all fighting men and women regardless of how many times they've heard the terrifying sounds of battle.

Do you remember the movie *Saving Private Ryan*? American landing craft were approaching Omaha Beach on the Normandy Coast during World War II. Army Ranger Captain John Miller (played by Tom Hanks) was noticeably nervous and concerned. Miller was older and more mature than most of his men. Most were citizen-soldiers, not professional (career) warriors. Unlike the other men in the landing craft, Miller had already experienced a murderous beach assault and was well aware of the death and mayhem that awaited his men ashore.

Saving Private Ryan was actually based on true events. Dr. Stephen Ambrose, author of *D-Day: The Climactic Battle of World War II*, also noted that the inexperience and naivety of the young Americans assaulting the Normandy Coast was considered a positive thing by Army planners because they didn't know what they'd really be facing. But were they scared? They wouldn't have been normal if they weren't!

Still, it takes a few courageous trained men in each group to mobilize the remaining troops and direct them to carry out their mission. Their courage helps the others to move beyond their fears when the natural inclination is to run for their lives.

"There are no great men, only great challenges that ordinary men are forced by circumstances to meet."
Fleet Admiral William F. Halsey, Jr., U.S. Navy

Necessity sometimes compels men and women to act heroically. James Michener in his 1953 novel (and movie of the same title) about the Korean War, *The Bridges of Toko Ri*, observed that circumstances can become a driving factor in making a person courageous. Navy fighter pilot, Lieutenant Harry Brubaker (played by William Holden in the 1955 movie), is shot down after a bombing mission in North Korea. The helicopter rescue pilot, Chief Mike Forney (played by Mickey Rooney), is also shot down while attempting to rescue Brubaker. While hiding in a ditch surrounded by enemy troops, Brubaker tells Forney, "You fight because you're there."

A little courage by both Brubaker and Forney seemed to sustain them both as they continued to defend themselves against a North Korean patrol. They were greatly outnumbered and their ultimate demise was short in coming, but their last moments were not of despair but of defiance.

> ## "Necessity does the work of courage."
> **George Eliot**

Summary of Key Points

- Courage is contagious.
- A few courageous trained men in each group can help other team members be courageous.
- Necessity may compel people to be courageous.

27

The Courage to Motivate

Courageous leaders motivate their followers with enthusiasm, encouragement, generosity, and praise. Enthusiasm is the strong excitement of feelings. Leaders are passionate about what they do and about the people with whom they do it. The most exceptional leaders, like Bill Gates, take passion up to a higher level. Gates believes, "What I do best is share my enthusiasm."

Kay Jamison's 2004 book, *Exuberance: the Passion for Life*, explores exuberance and its manifestations of joyful energy, vitality, excitement, and positive feelings. Examples of exuberant leaders are Theodore Roosevelt, John Muir, and Winston Churchill. We can think of exuberance as being joyously enthusiastic or possessing amplified enthusiasm.

What is the source of this positive energy? Each of us possesses a genius in some area. Other people may have a few areas where they perform at a high level. When we operate in our genius arena, we can be exuberant. We feel creative, joyous, and energized.

> **"Genius is talent set on fire by courage."**
> Henry van Dyke

Sir Patrick Moore has perhaps done more to popularize astronomy than any person alive. His monthly BBC television show is still on the air—over 50 years and running. When he turned 80 years old in 2003, he wrote an autobiography entitled, *Eighty Not Out*. I can only imagine how many people have become excited about astronomy because of Patrick's passion for the subject.

> **"Life shrinks or expands
> in proportion to one's courage."**
> Anaïs Nin

Patrick Moore is exuberant about astronomy. It shows in every facet of his life. It defines who he is. And like courage, exuberance is also contagious. What are you truly passionate about?

Effective leaders are encouraging as well. Look at the word "encouragement." As noted earlier, it means to give courage, hope, and spirit to others.

Offering Encouragement

- Leaders do this best in person with their words and deeds. If not in person, be creative—voice mail, text messages, e-mails, Post-It notes, handwritten letters or notes, postcards, etc.

- Leaders create an environment in which their followers will want to follow them. It builds a person's self-esteem, promotes a positive attitude, and validates a relationship.

- Leaders can encourage their followers by acknowledgment, affirmation, or appreciation of their efforts.

- Leaders don't minimize the negative but emphasize the positive. Their hope in the future is not wishful thinking but rather confident expectation.

- Effective leaders do not delegate encouragement down the chain of command.

- Leaders insist that everyone below them in the leadership chain also encourage their people.

- Leaders empower their people with enthusiasm to take a firm stand in the face of opposition.

Effective leaders are also generous. Churchill believed, "Generosity is always wise." If he could be magnanimous to vanquished political and military foes, how much more should we be to our loyal followers? Leaders ask and often demand a great deal from their people, but leadership is not just a one way street. The special relationship between leaders and followers means leaders should not be stingy with their encouragement.

With their words leaders lubricate the wheels of leadership and fortify their followers. If encouragement is the spark that keeps organizations energized, then praise is the fuel that propels workers to give their best efforts.

Effective Praise Must Be:

- Appropriate
- Timely
- Specific
- Consistent
- Sincere
- Enthusiastic
- Public

All too often, praise is as rare as a grand slam in the World Series. People have jokingly indicated the only time they have heard their boss say "well done" was when ordering a steak!

Praise has the quality of not being used up. That is, to give some of it away does not deplete its source. If you give a person a piece of pie, eventually, the pie will be completely consumed. Not so with praise. Of course, capricious, unceasing, and general praise dilute the value of the praise.

Effective praise is best when fresh—as close to the events or circumstances that precipitated it as possible. As memories fade, praise ceases to produce good feelings.

The more specific the praise, the better. "Good job" or "well done" misses the target and tends to come across as hollow and insincere. By being more specific and praising in public helps to reinforce the values that you seek to promote. (It is also best to criticize or reprimand someone in private.)

Courageous leaders realize that motivating their people is their most fundamental responsibility. It is not something delegated to a chief of staff or administrative assistant. Leaders keep their hand on this rudder.

Summary of Key Points

- Leaders motivate their followers with enthusiasm, encouragement, and generosity.
- Leaders encourage, that is, give courage to their people.
- Leaders should not be stingy with their encouragement.
- Effective praise will lubricate the wheels of leadership.

28

The Landscape of Leadership

The shifting sands of the Sahara probably represent better the nature of leadership than the granite peaks of the Himalayas. Today's landscape of leadership has become more:

- Dynamic and situational
- Sophisticated and technical
- Complex and multivariable
- Rapidly changing and nonlinear
- Global and networked

All leaders need to act courageously. But action alone isn't enough! The action needs to be appropriate, focused, and sustained. Focus implies assuming responsibility and accountability for the actions taken. Leaders bring a solution-oriented attitude to everything they do. Please see Appendix B for "A Message to Garcia," a celebrated and classic example of being action oriented.

Whenever I walk into the business section of a bookstore, I'm overwhelmed with the number of books on the shelves about leadership. We can find books that contain the leadership secrets of everyone from Attila the Hun, to Abraham Lincoln, to Wendy's Dave Thomas. We can find books about leadership that is invented, reinvented, visionary, strategic, servant, maximized, charismatic, innovative, intuitive, breakthrough, courageous, creative, enlightened and victorious. Or we can have our leadership by the numbers: the seven habits (Covey later added an eighth habit), the fourteen points (Deming), the twenty-one irrefutable laws (Maxwell). All these books and the programs they represent are extremely valuable. People, however, need a simpler system to learn what really matters most about leadership.

The Churchillian approach of vision, courage, and determination gives us a sound means to capture the essence of leadership. These three factors are a package, not fruit that is gathered and employed individually. The three synergize. Vision without courage and determination leads to hopelessness—you see it, but you don't believe you can get it! Courage without vision and determination leads to tilting at windmills, taking on too many tasks and challenges that lead nowhere. Finally, determination without vision and courage makes us rigid, dogmatic, and more likely to place blame for our lack of progress on others.

We can distill leadership even further into two fundamental words: "Follow me!" This is the quintessence of leadership. A leader needs the courage to lead by example, that is, from the front not the rear. An effective leader knows the importance of his or her presence among the followers. And if leadership by example is the watchword, then leadership by paperwork or leadership by meetings is anathema. To solve problems, leaders mobilize and motivate their people in person, not by memo.

Leadership is a dynamic relationship between the leader and the followers who are joined by common goals. What may surprise many is the delicate balance found in this relationship. Leadership is a gift given to the leaders by the followers because the followers give the leaders permission to lead.

Leaders and followers, like matter and energy, are two forms of the same thing. Furthermore, leaders sometimes follow, and followers sometimes lead. During a shipboard crisis such as fire, flooding, or personnel injury, the first person discovering the problem might initially be in charge of the recovery efforts. Effective training and cross training thus create a pool of potential leaders who can respond when needed.

Many businesses today still rely on antiquated ideas concerning leadership. Some still believe in the autocratic leader at the top who gives direction (uncontested orders) to those below. The command, control, and coercion model of leadership, however, has evolved into more decentralized approaches embodying elements of Transformational Leadership (Burns), Situational Leadership (Blanchard and Hersey), Action Centered Leadership (Adair), Servant Leadership (Greenleaf), and others.

Some executives do not have a clear picture of the differences between a leader and a manager. Without belaboring the many differences between them that can be found in current primers about leadership, two important distinctions should be mentioned. First, managers are appointed but leaders are chosen. Second, management is a subset of leadership and not the other way round. An effective leader is also a competent manager.

We can measure a leader's effectiveness by the success he or she achieves in accomplishing the commonly held goals. A leader places himself at risk of being rejected, ridiculed, and rebuffed by those who aren't under the microscope of public scrutiny and uncertain success.

Since a leadership potential exists at every level of our organizations, we have two critical responsibilities:

1. To develop the leadership potential that exists throughout the business or organization by creating a reservoir of leaders, prospective leaders, and active followers.

2. To tap into the talents, creativity, and energy of every person in the business or organization.

> **"The true task of leadership is not to put greatness into humanity, but to elicit it, since the greatness is already there."**
> **John Buchan**

Theodore Roosevelt was an extraordinarily talented leader. He knew great achievements as well as criticism. He seemed to shoulder disapproval by others with aplomb. He said, "The credit belongs to the man who is actually in the arena, whose face is marred by dust and sweat and blood, who strives valiantly, who errs and comes up short again and again, because there is no effort without error or shortcoming, but who knows the great enthusiasms, the great devotions, who spends himself for a worthy cause; who, at the best, knows, in the end, the triumph of high achievement, and who, at the worst, if he fails, at least he fails while daring greatly, so that his place shall never be with those cold and timid souls who knew neither victory nor defeat."

> **"Whatever course you decide upon, there is always someone to tell you that you are wrong. There are always difficulties arising which tempt you to believe that your critics are right. To map out a course of action and follow it to the end requires courage."**
> **Ralph Waldo Emerson**

In former times, the word *élan*, that is, vigorous spirit or enthusiasm, was an attribute courageous leaders possessed. *Élan* is an appropriate word that should be resurrected in our lexicon.

Leaders also need to exhibit what Admiral Mike Mullen would call an "undaunted commitment" to their mission. Undaunted, that is fearless, is another word that should be restored to our vocabulary.

A leader remains a force-multiplier in any organization. Both Napoleon III and Charles Maurine de Talleyrand have evoked this belief, citing an ancient proverb that "an army of sheep commanded by a lion would defeat an army of lions led by a sheep."

Leaders have a solemn responsibility to guide, mold, and nurture the leaders of the future. They leave their understudies, as Frederick Buechner would, "maybe even wiser and with something more of honor, of courage, of the resolve ... to do something with the rest of their lives that might ease the world's pain a little ..."

There are no shortcuts to becoming a leader. It's a life-long journey punctuated by trials and tribulations. And it takes nothing less than a total commitment to forging one's character with courage.

Summary of Key Points

- Leadership which can be described as vision, courage, and determination can be further distilled to "follow me."
- Leaders and followers, like matter and energy, are two forms of the same thing.
- Leaders are committed to developing the entire leadership potential that exists in their organizations.
- Leaders continue to press on with *élan* and "undaunted commitment" to their mission.

29

Courageous Leaders

Today's leaders are called upon to leap tall buildings in a single bound, perform miracles, and use magical powers to solve unsolvable problems—that's why they get paid the big bucks! Honestly, we put a great deal of responsibility on the shoulders of our leaders. This is because effective leaders:

- Make difficult decisions.
- Take balanced risks.
- Lead from the front not the rear.
- Do not confine themselves to the solutions of the past.
- Set the standard for honesty and integrity by taking morally appropriate actions.
- Respond to a crisis with strength, confidence, poise, and calmness.

- Mo iva e followers wi h en husiasm, encourage-
men , generosi y, and praise especially during
periods of adversi y, hardship, and suffering.

- Do no le fear cap ure he minds and s ampede
he spiri s of heir followers.

- Are able o make he dis inc ion be ween
courage and i s absence. When hey recognize
courage is missing, hey fill in he gap.

- Keep hope alive.

"Valor is a gift. Those having it never know
for sure whether they have it till the test
comes. And those having it in one test
never know for sure if they will have it
when the next test comes."
Carl Sandburg

In he Navy, des royers are considered he
workhorses of he flee . They are mul ipurpose warships
ha can comba enemy aircraf , surface ships,
submarines, and land arge s. They can opera e as par
of large ba le groups, in company wi h similar kinds of
vessels, escor convoys of merchan ships, or opera e
independen ly. Des royermen call heir ships " in cans"
because hey have rela ively sligh armor pro ec ion
compared o he heavy cruisers and ba leships of
bygone eras. Tin-can sailors are renowned for heir "can
do" a i ude!

In our organiza ions oday, here are wo kinds of
people: hose who are "can do" and hose who are "no can
do." The favori e word of he "no can do" people is *NO!*

No is the default setting for most responses. Sociologists tell us that by the time a person reaches eighteen, they have heard "no" over 300,000 times! That means we're conditioned to say "no" almost before we hear a question. When we work to create a win-win, mutually beneficial opportunity with other people, "no" is not a good starting point.

Leaders need to change the conversation for possibility in our work places and homes. Changing the way we speak may make a significant change in our impact and influence. Instead of saying what comes naturally, that is, "no," substitute the words, "That's a tough one. Let's see what we can do." Then the leader and the followers can brainstorm for opportunity and come up with a better solution for their problems. (Sometimes "no" is indeed the appropriate response but needs to be reexamined on a case-by-case basis.)

Courageous leaders and active followers are passionate about serving their customers. "Can do" people bring value to their clients. They do this in one of four ways:

- Can they *identify* problems?
- Can they *solve* problems?
- Can they *anticipate* problems?
- Can they *prevent* problems?

The most basic level entails identifying problems. A more professional "can do" person will help solve problems. The most valuable "can do" person helps to anticipate and prevent problems. At which level do you work? At which level can you work? Do you see how you can be more valuable to your organization, your customers, and your customers' customers?

"Can do" leaders possess unshakable integrity and do what is right. Their moral compass calibrates their entire organization.

> ## "Men don't follow titles.
> ## They follow courage."
> **William Wallace to Robert Bruce in *Braveheart***

Think about Olympic athletes. They are the best at what they do yet they strive to be a little better. There are three steps in this process: practice, practice, and more practice! Olympic athletes are fanatical believers in continuous improvement. For those of us who aren't the best at what we do, practice becomes an even more important challenge.

Olympic athletes have coaches to help them improve still further. They have performance coaches, nutrition coaches, psychological coaches, sports medicine coaches, etc. Each of us would also benefit from a coach or coaches.

Who would make a good coach for you? Start with the people around you: your spouse, a parent, a grandparent, a supervisor at work, a co-worker, a friend, a pastor, a role model in your career field, a mentor, or a professional coach. If we want to push the envelope in our lives and be more than we ever imagined becoming, coaches can help.

Each of us is in the Olympics of our lives. This is it! This is your life! As Werner Erhard used to say, "What is, is. What isn't, isn't."

In the game of life there are three important realities:

1. The clock is always running!

2. There are no timeouts!

3. There is no time to lose!

Dr. James C. Denison accurately noted, "Urgency breeds courage. And the enemy of courage is complacency." We can start today by living our lives like an Olympian. We can instill a sense of urgency and enthusiasm into the time we have left on this planet. If we have a clear sense of purpose and the commitment to live life to the fullest, we can boldly propel ourselves to exciting new possibilities. And isn't this the essence of what cultivating courage is all about?

Summary of Key Points

- "Can do" people bring significant value to their organizations by identifying, solving, anticipating, and preventing problems.
- Benchmarking best practices of Olympic athletes with respect to practice and coaching will enhance a person's effectiveness and achievement.
- To be courageous means recognizing that there is sense of urgency to what we do.

30

Being Forehanded

Forehandedness is a U.S. Navy term that refers to anticipating future situations and thinking about how to deal appropriately with them. The tenth edition of the *U.S. Navy Watch Officer's Guide* suggests, "Always look ahead, a minute, an hour, or a day, and make it your pride never to be caught unprepared. Rehearse mentally the actions you would take in the event of a fire, man overboard, a steering failure, or any other serious casualty. This habit is not difficult to acquire and is certain to pay large dividends over the course of years. Forehandedness is the mark of the successful man in any capacity."

> **"Great things are done more through courage than through wisdom."**
> **German proverb**

When I was in grade school, I remember my dad giving me a book entitled, *On Your Toes in Baseball*. As a Little League outfielder, I was encouraged to think about where a ball might be hit on the field and give some forethought as to what actions I would take.

When I worked for the Defense Nuclear Agency on Oahu, Hawaii, I participated in various nuclear safety drills that were based on some worst-case scenarios. In one exercise our response hinged on having adequate communications available to get the word out to all the necessary players. We made sure we had sufficient dedicated telephone numbers and backup numbers promulgated to all the right people. We had detailed checklists that covered everything from soup to nuts. Nothing seemed left to chance.

One year later, a tsunami warning initiated by an earthquake off Alaska resulted in some massive emergency actions in the low-lying areas of Oahu, including the heavy tourist area of Waikiki. The high volume of calls to and from these areas caused the entire telephone system to experience a gridlock. Had we experienced a nuclear safety problem, our principal means of communication would probably have been similarly thwarted. Our incorrect assumption was that the telephone system would function as normal. It didn't. Our planning was, therefore, inadequate!

No one can anticipate every possible situation or problem especially when the number of variables exceeds our mind's ability to process. Being forehanded may help us prevent from being caught by surprise—a source of fear. And preparing for difficult situations in advance may help us recover our poise and focus when we are thrown a curve ball.

Cultivating courage is a conscious choice for each person. Those who aspire to become even more effective leaders will meet this opportunity with discipline and dedication.

The new demands on our leaders grow each day. The challenges they face defy imagination. The consequences of ineffective leadership are not just frightening but also unforgiving! Global terrorism, weapons of mass destruction, genetic engineering, human-accelerated global warming, and regional genocide are terrible legacies that we leave behind to our children and grandchildren.

We can, however, leave a more enduring and positive bequest of courageous and victorious leadership! The crux of this book is this: We do not need more information. We need more courage! When we analyze the source of a person's failure, we discover (as did St. Ignatius of Loyola some five hundred years ago) not a lack of intellect, but rather a lack of will.

> **"No matter what mark an officer may leave in history by his deeds in battle, or in intellectual contributions, or in material inventions, his greatest legacy to his country will be the example he has given as a man and as a leader of men."**
> **Admiral Arleigh Burke, U.S. Navy**

We no longer have the luxury of just muddling through. The hopes and dreams of free men and women all around this planet hinge on courageous leaders doing the right things at the right time.

In leadership there simply is no substitute for courage. And never in the history of the human race has the need for courageous leaders been greater! The stakes are high. When the time comes, will we be ready?

Summary of Key Points

- Being forehanded helps prevent being surprised—a source of fear.
- We do not need more information. We just need more courage!
- One of the greatest legacies a person can leave is that of a leader of men and women.

31

The Five Cornerstones Redux

The Five Cornerstones of Courage™ give us a comprehensive view of the nature of courage. They provide us tools needed to slay the giants that stand between us and our desired outcomes.

Let's see these five elements together:

> ## Five Cornerstones of Courage™
>
> 1. Courage is taking action despite fear.
> 2. Courage grows out of clarity of purpose.
> 3. Courage is like a muscle.
>   We can develop it by using it.
> 4. Courage resides in everyone.
> 5. Courage is contagious.

These strategies, techniques, approaches and insights to cultivate courage can help us to prepare ourselves to be ready when the situation arises:

- Ten courage-building/fear-management strategies
- Ten balanced risk-taking strategies
- Ten strategies to conquer procrastination
- 7-17-27 Stairstep Approach™
- Sixteen focus and concentration techniques
- Four domains for stepping outside comfort zones
- Five more ambitious stretches
- One Plus Technique™
- Eight changes of perspective
- Benchmarking heroes and role models
- Exercising patience
- Using creativity
- Getting stronger physically
- Remembering past successes
- Four ways to build boldness
- Destroyermen's Approach™
- Seven encouragement and praise techniques
- Ten attributes of courageous leaders
- Four ways "can do" people add value
- Developing forehandedness

> **"What gives us courage is believing what we want is achievable."**
> **Naomi Kryske**

We were all naturally courageous, once. When we were children, it didn't occur to us that we could fail. We'd take great risks. We learned to walk. We learned to ride a bicycle. We learned to climb trees, and we'd sometimes climb out on a limb.

As we grew up, we grew more and more cautious. We were taught that we could fail. And unfortunately we bought into this idea.

This belief in failure has been a great weight that has pulled us down. It has held us back. It has robbed us of our happiness and our vitality. We must rediscover the spirit of our childhood. We *can* lead courageous lives both at work and at home.

If I Were Brave—A song © **Jana Stanfield**

What would I do, if I knew that I could not fail?
If I believed, would the wind always fill up my sail?
How far would I go? What could I achieve,
trusting the hero in me?

If I were brave, I'd walk the razor's edge,
where fools and dreamers dare to tread.
I'd never lose faith, even when losing my way.
What step would I take today, if I were brave?

What would I do today, if I were brave?
What would I do today, if I were brave?

What if we're all meant to do what we secretly dream?
What would you ask, if you knew you could have anything?
Like the mighty oak sleeps, in the heart of a seed,
are there miracles in you and me?

If I were brave, I'd walk the razor's edge,
where fools and dreamers dare to tread.
I'd never lose faith, even when losing my way.
What step would I take today, if I were brave?

What would I do today, if I were brave?
What would I do today, if I were brave?

If I refuse to listen to the voice of fear,
would the voice of courage whisper in my ear?

If I were brave, I'd walk the razor's edge,
where fools and dreamers dare to tread.
I'd never lose faith, even when losing my way.
What step would I take today, if I were brave?

What would I do today, if I were brave?
What would I do today, if I were brave?

> **"To challenge the fates, that is living! To ride the storm, to live daringly, to live nobly, not wasting one's life in foolish and silly risks ..."**
> **Louis L'Amour**

It has been asked: Since David the shepherd knew that God was on his side, why did he pick up five smooth stones instead of just one? Whatever the answer, the more important issue is that David "ran quickly" at his adversary. He faced his challenge head on and without delay. That's courage!

Summary of Key Points

- The Five Cornerstones of Courage and the associated strategies, techniques, insights, and approaches, can help people cultivate courage and prepare themselves to be ready when the situation arises.
- We must rediscover the spirit of our childhood. We *can* lead courageous lives both at work and at home.
- Face challenges head on and without delay. That's courage!

32

Ready, BEGIN!

1957 was an extremely formative year for Americans. It was the year Sputnik scared us into a race to space with the Soviet Union. We watched *Leave it to Beaver* and the *Bridge on the River Kwai*. We ate Pez and read Dr. Seuss' *Cat in the Hat*. We played with hula hoops and started seeing strange automobiles made by Toyota on our streets. We paid only 3 cents to mail a letter and in a thousand-and-one-nights kingdom called Saudi Arabia a baby named Osama Bin Laden was born.

1957 was also the year of my first speaking engagement. I was a quiet, shy, obedient second grader in Miss Cassidy's class at Grandview Boulevard School in West Lost Angeles.

Just after arithmetic, one of my favorite subjects, Miss Cassidy stopped by my desk. "Larry, would you please wait after class a minute?" I looked up at her. She towered over me, but so did every adult. I was only eight. "I want to talk with you about something."

"Yes, Miss Cassidy," I answered weakly.

Oh no. What did I do wrong? I'm in for it now. Could Miss Cassidy have seen the note I passed to Bobby? I did it two weeks ago. Maybe she forgot all about it and then something just reminded her of it again. And what will Mom think? She's waiting in the car for me. She'll be mad if I'm late. I sure don't want Dad to find out about this!

I felt dread in my stomach. I racked my brain trying to see if there were something else bad I had done. *I threw away the squished peanut butter sandwich I brought to school yesterday. Did I miss the trash can? Maybe that was it. And I think I stopped running when I heard the bell signaling the end of recess. I'm sure I walked without talking back to my classroom. It must be the note. Did Bobby squeal on me? I thought he was my friend. That's the last time I'll try to help him out.*

The rest of the school day passed slowly. It seemed like I looked up at the clock above the blackboard every few seconds. Finally, the bell rang and Miss Cassidy dismissed the class. Everyone except me, that is. I waited nervously while she tidied up her desk. Then she motioned for me to come over to her. Like a frightened mouse, I tiptoed over to her desk.

"Larry, tomorrow is Friday, and we'll have an assembly in the auditorium in the morning for all classes. I'd like you to lead us in the Pledge of Allegiance." I gulped and looked closely at her. She didn't look angry. She had a warm, pleasant, inviting face. I actually liked her, much more than the teacher I'd had for first grade. "See you tomorrow," she smiled as she dismissed me.

Now I was in for it. Maybe she didn't see the note I gave Bobby, but I was in hotter water. She wants me to lead the Pledge tomorrow? In front of the whole school?

There have to be over a thousand students at an assembly! Well, maybe only five hundred. But I hate getting up in front of just my class, and it's only twenty! What am I to do? Why would Miss Cassidy do this to me?

I didn't tell my parents. I was too appalled. I was a quiet person. I liked to spend time by myself with my stamp collection or catching lizards or reading. Now I was going to have to be out in front of everyone. I could see all those faces staring back at me. Would they laugh at my jeans? I told Mom the cuffs were too high! Now everyone will know.

What if I forget to say the right words? I remember hearing some sixth grader at the last assembly. Her voice seemed strong and confident. "Everyone please rise and repeat after me the Pledge of Allegiance to the United States of America." I tried to practice the words but the more I did, the more jumbled up in my mind they became. I didn't sleep well that night.

The next morning I didn't feel like eating breakfast. When Dad wasn't looking, I hid my toast in my pocket. Mom dropped me off at school and wished me a good day. She didn't have a clue what my day would be like! I'd rather be going to the doctor. I should have pretended to be sick but I didn't really want one of those big shots I always got.

My class lined up behind Mrs. Elliot's class, and we walked without talking to the auditorium. I couldn't have said anything anyway—my throat was already tight. All the different classes converged on the auditorium. *Look at all those kids! Hundreds of them, and they'll all be looking at me. I can't even remember my name. Why did Miss Cassidy pick me? Harvey would have been a better choice—He's taller than I am. Or even*

Charlene—She's smarter, except in arithmetic, geography, and PE.

We walked inside the auditorium and were told to take our seats quietly. *No problem for me! Quiet was my middle name!* There was still a lot of commotion as kids whispered to their neighbors. More and more classes came in and took their seats. Miss Cassidy came over and tapped me on the shoulder. Like a robot, my legs moved, and I followed her onto the stage.

When I reached the top of the stage, Miss Cassidy noticed the frightened look on my face. She bent over and calmly whispered, "All you have to do is face the flag, put your hand over your heart, and say into the microphone 'Ready, begin.' They'll know what to do." My mouth was dry, and my hands were clammy.

The school principal, Miss Helder, motioned me to a seat. Miss Cassidy went to sit with our class. The assembly began with a brief welcome from the principal. She then said, "Larry Kryske from Miss Cassidy's class will now lead us in the Pledge of Allegiance." She looked at me.

I stood up. Time went into slow motion. My feet were glued to the floor. *Feet, move!* I somehow covered the five steps to the microphone. I glanced over the crowd. Everyone was quiet, too quiet. They were all looking at me. I placed my hand over my pounding heart. Mustering all the voice I had, I spoke in the microphone, "Ready, begin."

Miraculously, everyone knew what to do just as Miss Cassidy had said! A great weight lifted from my shoulders as I recited the Pledge. I was jubilant! I had done it!

Afterward when we were all back in our class, I asked Miss Cassidy, "Why me?"

She replied, "I thought you'd need to feel comfortable in front of an audience someday."

How did she know? In later years I've spoken to groups of seventy to seven hundred to seven thousand! I learned a powerful lesson that day in 1957: Courage is stepping out despite my fear.

The actions I took and the words I spoke that day are what we need to overcome our fears. All we need to do is symbolically place our hand over our heart, the icon of courage, and repeat to ourselves, "Ready, begin!"

Appendix A:

The Churchill Factors

The Churchill Factors—vision, courage, and determination—are simple ideas to understand but are not easy to achieve. Please do not confuse simple with simplistic. The former word means uncomplicated. The latter word means to reduce something falsely by assuming it is unsophisticated or one-dimensional.

Vision, courage, and determination are anything but simplistic! Actually, each element embodies several other characteristics. Mastery of the different elements requires discipline and practice. The good news is that a person can aspire to and become an effective leader.

Three problems plague business people: failure of imagination, failure of will, and failure to use time effectively. These three breakdowns prevent the desired outcomes that decision makers identify in their strategic planning sessions. The Churchill Factors address two of the three problems: failure of imagination (vision) and failure of will (courage and determination).

VISION
"If you can see it, you can paint it!"
What do I want to be, do, or have?

COURAGE
"Do it now, and don't look back!"
What do I need to do to get started?

DETERMINATION
"Never give in!"
How do I achieve my outcome?

"By our courage, our endurance, and our brains, we have made our way in the world to the lasting benefit of mankind. Let us not lose heart. Our future is one of high hope."
Winston S. Churchill

The matrix on the next page shows that each of the three Churchill Factors is actually composed of twelve subelements. It is as if vision, courage, and determination were a trinary star system. There are mutual gravitation attractions holding this stellar system together. When the light of each individual star is passed through a spectroscope, a different spectrum appears. Just as astronomers can determine the chemical composition of a stellar atmosphere from its spectrum, leaders can discern different subelements from vision, courage, and determination.

The Churchill Factors

VISION	COURAGE	DETERMINATION
Focus	Risk Taking	Tenacity
Innovation	Introspection	Resilience
Perspective	Enthusiasm	Problem Solving
Simplicity	Generosity	Attitude
Being Proactive	Priorities/Timing	Discipline
Open Minded	Integrity/Truth	Dedication
Insightful	Decision Making	Action Oriented
Adding Value	Judgment	Patience
Detail Oriented	Empathy	Versatility
Big Picture	Accountability	Involving Others
Discernment	Loyalty	Impassioned
Preparation	Boldness	Flexibility

Winston Churchill's leadership style, therefore, is more than simply vision, courage, and determination. The Churchill Factors were merely the broad brush strokes that he cast upon his canvas. With smaller brushes he fleshed out the details involving focus, boldness, enthusiasm, generosity, resilience, and the like.

Vision, courage, and determination and their accompanying thirty-six subelements synergize and result in one of the most sought for but least achieved outcomes: VICTORY!

> "You ask: 'What is our aim?' I can answer in one word: It is victory, victory at all costs, victory in spite of all terror, victory however long and hard the road may be; for without victory there is no survival."
> Winston S. Churchill

Appendix B:

A Message to Garcia

In Fall, 1972, my first ship, *USS Parsons (DDG 33)*, had just returned to our homeport of Yokosuka, Japan, following a forty-day period on the gunline off the demilitarized zone that separated North from South Vietnam. I had asked the Executive Officer a question concerning some tasking he had given me. Rather than answer, he handed me a copy of Elbert Hubbard's essay, "A Message to Garcia."

The essay described an officer of great initiative and resourcefulness. I later learned that Hubbard's work was a classic piece given to enlistees during both World War One and World War Two. It was written in 1899. The setting was the Cuba, then a Spanish colony, soon to be a battleground in the Spanish-American War in 1898.

The protagonist of the story was Andrew Summers Rowan, an 1881 graduate of the U.S. Military Academy at West Point. Calixto Garcia was a Cuban freedom fighter. The Americans were planning their invasion of Cuba and desired to coordinate their actions with the Cuban insurgents.

"A Message to Garcia" was allegedly written in one hour after supper. It became one of the most widely read essays in the America prior to the Second World War, but succeeding generations of business people have never read it.

A sad postscript accompanies Hubbard's enthusiastic essay. He and his wife died when the *RMS Lusitania* was torpedoed by German submarine *U-20* in 1915 off Ireland. The ship was en route from England to Germany on a mission to end the war. Almost 1,200 of the 2,000 passengers and crew perished after the huge four-stack ocean liner sank in just eighteen minutes.

> **"The difference between getting somewhere and nowhere is the courage to make an early start."**
> **Charles M. Schwab**

A Message to Garcia

By Elbert Hubbard

In all this Cuban business there is one man who stands out on the horizon of my memory like Mars at perihelion.

When war broke out between Spain & the United States, it was very necessary to communicate quickly with the leader of the Insurgents. Garcia was somewhere in the mountain vastness of Cuba no one knew where. No mail nor telegraph message could reach him. The President must secure his cooperation, and quickly.

What to do!

Some one said to the President, "There's a fellow by the name of Rowan will find Garcia for you, if anybody can."

Rowan was sent for and given a letter to be delivered to Garcia. How "the fellow by the name of Rowan" took the letter, sealed it up in an oil-skin pouch, strapped it over his heart, in four days landed by night off the coast of Cuba from an open boat, disappeared into the jungle, and in three weeks came out on the other side of the Island, having traversed a hostile country on foot, and delivered his letter to Garcia, are things I have no special desire now to tell in detail.

The point I wish to make is this: McKinley gave Rowan a letter to be delivered to Garcia; Rowan took the letter and did not ask, "Where is he?"

By the Eternal! There is a man whose form should be cast in deathless bronze and the statue placed in every college of the land. It is not book-learning young men need, nor instruction about this and that, but a stiffening of the vertebrae which will cause them to be loyal to a trust, to act promptly, concentrate their energies: do the thing- "Carry a message to Garcia!"

General Garcia is dead now, but there are other Garcias. No man, who has endeavored to carry out an enterprise where many hands were needed, has been well nigh appalled at times by the imbecility of the average man—the inability or unwillingness to concentrate on a thing and do it.

Slip-shod assistance, foolish inattention, dowdy indifference, and half-hearted work seem the rule; and no man succeeds, unless by hook or crook, or threat, he forces or bribes other men to assist him; or mayhap, God in His goodness performs a miracle, & sends him an Angel of Light for an assistant.

You, reader, put this matter to a test: You are sitting now in your office—six clerks are within call. Summon any one and make this request: "Please look in the encyclopedia and make a brief memorandum for me concerning the life of Correggio". Will the clerk quietly say, "Yes, sir," and go do the task?

On your life, he will not. He will look at you out of a fishy eye and ask one or more of the following questions: Who was he? Which encyclopedia? Where is the encyclopedia? Was I hired for that? Don't you mean Bismarck? What's the matter with Charlie doing it? Is he dead? Is there any hurry? Shan't I bring you the book and let you look it up yourself? What do you want to know for?

And I will lay you ten to one that after you have answered the questions, and explained how to find the information, and why you want it, the clerk will go off and get one of the other clerks to help him try to find Garcia- and then come back and tell you there is no such man. Of course I may lose my bet, but according to the Law of Averages, I will not.

Now if you are wise you will not bother to explain to your "assistant" that Correggio is indexed under the C's, not in the K's, but you will smile sweetly and say, "Never mind," and go look it up yourself. And this incapacity for independent action, this moral stupidity, this infirmity of the will, this unwillingness to cheerfully catch hold and lift, are the things that put pure Socialism so far into the future. If men will not act for themselves, what will they do when the benefit of their effort is for all?

A first-mate with knotted club seems necessary; and the dread of getting "the bounce" Saturday night, holds many a worker to his place. Advertise for a stenographer, and nine out of ten who apply, can neither spell nor punctuate—and do not think it necessary to.

Can such a one write a letter to Garcia?

"You see that bookkeeper," said the foreman to me in a large factory. "Yes, what about him?" "Well he's a fine accountant, but if I'd send him up town on an errand, he might accomplish the errand all right, and on the other hand, might stop at four saloons on the way, and when he got to Main Street, would forget what he had been sent for." Can such a man be entrusted to carry a message to Garcia?

We have recently been hearing much maudlin sympathy expressed for the "downtrodden denizen of the sweat-shop" and the "homeless wanderer searching for honest employment," and with it all often go many hard words for the men in power.

Nothing is said about the employer who grows old before his time in a vain attempt to get frowsy ne'er-do-wells to do intelligent work; and his long patient striving with "help" that does nothing but loaf when his back is turned.

In every store and factory there is a constant weeding-out process going on. The employer is constantly sending away "help" that have shown their incapacity to further the interests of the business, and others are being taken on. No matter how good times are, this sorting continues, only if times are hard and work is scarce, the sorting is done finer- but out and forever out, the incompetent and unworthy go. It is the survival of the fittest. Self-interest prompts every employer to keep the best—those who can carry a message to Garcia.

I know one man of really brilliant parts who has not the ability to manage a business of his own, and yet who is absolutely worthless to any one else, because he carries with him constantly the insane suspicion that his employer is oppressing, or intending to oppress him. He cannot give orders; and he will not receive them. Should a message be given him to take to Garcia, his answer would probably be, "Take it yourself."

Tonight this man walks the streets looking for work, the wind whistling through his threadbare coat. No one who knows him dare employ him, for he is a regular firebrand of discontent. He is impervious to reason, and the only thing that can impress him is the toe of a thick-soled No. 9 boot.

Of course I know that one so morally deformed is no less to be pitied than a physical cripple; but in our pitying, let us drop a tear, too, for the men who are striving to carry on a great enterprise, whose working hours are not limited by the whistle, and whose hair is fast turning white through the struggle to hold in line dowdy indifference, slip-shod imbecility, and the heartless ingratitude, which, but for their enterprise, would be both hungry & homeless.

Have I put the matter too strongly? Possibly I have; but when all the world has gone a-slumming I wish to speak a word of sympathy for the man who succeeds- the man who, against great odds has directed the efforts of others, and having succeeded, finds there's nothing in it: nothing but bare board and clothes. I have carried a dinner pail & worked for day's wages, and I have also been an employer of labor, and I know there is something to be said on both sides.

There is no excellence, per se, in poverty; rags are no recommendation; & all employers are not rapacious and high-handed, any more than all poor men are virtuous. My heart goes out to the man who does his work when the "boss" is away, as well as when he is at home. And the man who, when given a letter for Garcia, quietly take the missive, without asking any idiotic questions, and with no lurking intention of chucking it into the nearest sewer, or of doing aught else but deliver it, never gets "laid off," nor has to go on a strike for higher wages.

Civilization is one long anxious search for just such individuals. Anything such a man asks shall be granted; his kind is so rare that no employer can afford to let him go. He is wanted in every city, town and village—in every office, shop, store and factory. The world cries out for such: he is needed, and needed badly—the man who can carry a message to Garcia.

Appendix C:

Suggested Books about Courage

Ambrose, Stephen
D-Day June 6, 1944: The Climactic Battle of World War II (1994)
Band of Brothers. E Company, 506th Regiment, 101st Airborne (1992)
Nothing Like It in the World: The Men Who Built the Transcontinental
    Railroad 1863-1869 (2000)

Beschloss, Michael
Presidential Courage: Brave Leaders and How They Changed America
    1789-1989 (2007)

Brinkley, Douglas
The Great Deluge: Hurricane Katrina, New Orleans, and the Mississippi
    Gulf Coast (2006)

Burton, E. Milby
The Siege of Charleston 1861-1865 (1970)

Churchill, Sir Winston S.
My Early Life: A Roving Commission (1930)
The Second World War Volume 1: The Gathering Storm (1948)
The World Crisis Volume 2 (1923)

Clark, Allen
Wounded Soldier, Healing Warrior (2007)

Escamilla, Paul L.
Longing for Enough in a Culture of More (2007)

Gilbert, Sir Martin
Churchill: A Life (1991)
Winston Churchill: The Wilderness Years (1982)
In Search of Churchill: A Historian's Journey (1994)

Hackworth, David H. and Eilhys England
Steel My Soldiers' Hearts (2002)

Halberstam, David
Firehouse (2002)
The Coldest Winter: America and the Korean War (2007)

Harringan, Stephen
The Gates of the Alamo: A Novel (2000)

Hugo, Victor
Ninety-Three: A Novel (1988)

Johnson, Paul
Heroes: From Alexander the Great and Julius Caesar to Churchill
    and de Gaulle (2007)

Krakauer, Jon
Into Thin Air (1997)

Lukacs, John
Five Days in London: May 1940 (1999)

Manchester, William
The Last Lion Winston Spencer Churchill: Visions of Glory 1874-1932
    (1983)
The Last Lion Winston Spencer Churchill: Alone 1932-1040 (1988)
American Caesar: Douglas MacArthur 1880-1964 (1978)

McCain, John and Mark Salter
Why Courage Matters (2004)
Hard Call: Great Decisions and the Extraordinary People Who Made
    Them (2007)

Millard, Candice
Theodore Roosevelt Darkest Journey: The River of Doubt (2005)

Prochnau, William
Once Upon a Distant War: Reporting from Vietnam (1996)

Rand, Ayn
Atlas Shrugged: A Novel (1957)

Reisner, Marc
Cadillac Desert: The American West and Its Disappearing Water (1993)

Sandys, Celia
Churchill Wanted Dead or Alive (1999)

Salisbury, Gay and Laney Salisbury
The Cruelest Miles: The Heroic Story of Dogs and Men in a Race
    Against an Epidemic (2003)

Solzhenitsyn, Aleksandr
The Gulag Archipelago (1973)

Stockdale, James Bond and Sybil Stockdale
In Love and War: The Story of a Family's Ordeal and Sacrifice during the
    Vietnam Years (1984)

Stone, Irving
Depths of Glory: A Biographical Novel of Camille Pissarro (1985)

Warren, Stephen G.
Flying into Combat with Heroes (2003)

Wiesel, Elie
Night (1960)

Winters, Dick
Beyond the Band of Brothers: The War Memoirs of Major Dick Winters
    (2006)

Appendix D:

Suggested Movies
about Courage

Apollo 13: 1995, Tom Hanks, Crew nurses crippled spacecraft home.

Zulu: 1964, Michael Caine, 250 Brits hold off 4,000 Zulu warriors.

We Were Soldiers: Mel Gibson, 2001, Americans battle 3 days of hell in Ia Drang Valley in 1965.

Saving Private Ryan: 1998, Tom Hanks, D-Day at its worst and beyond.

Band of Brothers HBO series: 2001, Damian Lewis, Army company from D-Day to VE Day.

The Insider: 1999, Al Pacino, Russell Crowe, whistleblower warns of tobacco dangers.

United 93: 2006, Christian Clemenso, Passengers prevent terrorist skyjacking from succeeding.

Flags of Our Fathers: 2006, Ryan Phillippe, Heroism during Battle of Iwo Jima in WW2.

Twelve Angry Men: 1957, Henry Fonda, E.G. Marshall, One juror's courage to stand for justice and the rule of law in a murder trial.

Letters from Iwo Jima: 2006, Ken Watanabe, Heroism during Battle of Iwo Jima from the Japanese Perspective.

The Gathering Storm: 2003, Albert Finney, Churchill warns of Nazi menace.

The Great Escape: 1963, Steve McQueen, Mass escape from German POW camp in WW2.

Bridges of Toko Ri: 1955, William Holden, Grace Kelly, Carrier warfare during Korean War.

Glory: 1989, Morgan Freeman, Denzel Washington, Black soldiers attack fort near Charleston.

Naked Prey: 1966, Cornel Wilde, Safari leader captured, released, and hunted by natives.

Braveheart: 1995, Mel Gibson, William Wallace leads Scots to freedom from Brits.

Das Boot: 1981, Jurgen Prochnow, Tedium, fear, war on a U-boat in WW2.

Gandhi: 1982, Ben Kingsley, Non-violent revolt against British rule in India.

The Lost Battalion: 2001, Rick Schroder, Americans trapped behind enemy lines in WW1.

Battle of Britain: 1969, Michael Caine, Britain's famed Royal Air Force outnumbered.

The Alamo: 2004, Dennis Quaid, Recounts historic 13-day siege of the Alamo.

Backdraft: 1991, Kurt Russell, Chicago firefighters fight arsonist and themselves.

Mississippi Burning: 1988, Gene Hackman, FBI investigates missing civil rights workers.

Bibliography

Ambrose, Stephen. *Band of Brothers: E Company, 506th Regiment, 101st Airborne.* New York: Touchstone, 1992.

------ D-Day June 6th, 1944: The Climactic Battle of World War II. New York: Touchstone, 1995.

------ *Nothing Like It in the World: The Men Who Built the Transcontinental Railroad 1863-1869.* New York: Simon & Schuster, 2000.

------ *Undaunted Courage: Meriwether Lewis, Jefferson, and the Opening of the American West.* New York: Simon & Schuster, 1996.

Bibesco, Marrthe. *Sir Winston Churchill: Master of Courage.* London: Robert Hall, 1957.

Bass, Robert D. *Swamp Fox: The Life and Campaigns of General Francis Marion.* Orangeburg, SC: Sandlapper Publishing, 1974.

Beaglehole, J. C. *The Life of Captain James Cook.* Stanford, CA: Stanford University Press, 1974.

Blumenson, Martin. *The Patton Papers 1885-1940.* Boston: Houghton Mifflin Company, 1972.

------ *The Patton Papers 1940-1945.* Boston: Houghton Mifflin Co., 1974.

Bonds, Russell S. *Stealing the General: The Great Locomotive Chase and the First Medal of Honor.* Yardley, PA: Westholme Publishing, 2007.

Boorstein, Daniel J. *The Creators: A History of the Heroes of the Imagination.* New York: Random House, 1992.

------ *The Discoverers: A History of Man's Search to Know His World and Himself.* New York: Random House, 1983.

Botting, Douglas. *Dr. Eckener's Dream Machine: The Great Zeppelin and the Dawn of Air Travel.* New York: Henry Holt & Co., 2001.

Bradford, Ernle. A Wind from the North. New York: Harcourt, Brace & World, 1960.

------ *Siege: Malta 1940-1943.* New York: William Morrow and Company, 1986.

------ *The Great Siege.* New York: Harcourt, Brace & World, 1961.

Brands, H. W. *T. R. The Last Romantic.* New York: BasicBooks, 1997.

Brinkley, Douglas. *The Great Deluge: Hurricane Katrina, New Orleans, and the Mississippi Gulf Coast.* New York: Harper Collins Publishers, 2006.

Brown, Anthony Cave. *Bodyguard of Lies.* New York: Harper & Row Publishers, 1975.

Buchan, John. *The King's Grace: 1910-1935.* London: Hodder and Stoughton, 1935

Burton, E. Milby. *The Siege of Charleston 1861-1865.* Columbia, SC: University of South Carolina Press, 1970.

Carroll, Andrew (editor). *Behind the Lines: Powerful and Revealing American and Foreign War Letters.* New York: Scribner, 2006.

Chaffin, Tom. *Pathfinder: John Charles Fremont and the Course of American Empire.* New York: Hill and Wand, 2002.

Cherry-Garrard, Apsley. *The Worst Journey in the World.* New York: Carroll & Graf Publishers, 1989.

Churchill, Sir Winston S. *My Early Life: A Roving Commission*. London, Thornton Butterworth Limited, 1930.

------ *The Second World War Volume 1: The Gathering Storm*. Boston: Houghton Mifflin Company, 1948.

------ *The Second World War Volume 2: Their Finest Hour*. Boston: Houghton Mifflin Company, 1949.

------ *The World Crisis Volume 2*. New York: Chas Scribner's Sons, 1923.

Clark, Allen. *Wounded Soldier, Healing Warrior*. St. Paul, MN: Zenith Press, 2007.

Cope, Harley F. *Command at Sea: A Guide for the Naval Officer*. New York: W.W. Norton & Company, 1951.

Cousins, Norman. *Albert Schweitzer's Mission: Healing and Peace*. New York: W. W. Norton & Company, 1985.

------ *Anatomy of an Illness As Perceived by the Patient: Reflections on Healing and Regeneration*. New York: W.W. Norton & Company, 1979.

------ *Human Options: An Autobiographical Notebook*. New York: W.W. Norton & Company, 1981.

------ *The Healing Heart: Antidotes to Panic and Helplessness*. New York: W. W. Norton & Company, 1983.

Cross, Wilbur. *Disaster at the Pole: The Crash of the Airship Italia, Arctic Endurance and Survival*. Connecticut: Lyons Press, 2002.

Csikszentmihalyi, Mihaly. *Creativity: The Flow and the Psychology of Discovery and Invention*. New York: HarperCollins Publishers, 1996.

------ *Finding Flow: The Psychology of Engagement with Everyday Life*. New York: BasicBooks, 1997.

Davis, William C. *Three Roads to the Alamo: The Lives and Fortunes of David Crockett, James Bowie, and William Barret Travis*. New York: HarperCollins Publishers, 1998.

Deming, W. Edwards. *Out of the Crisis.* Cambridge, MA: Massachusetts Institute of Technology Center for Advanced Engineering Study, 1986.

Escamilla, Paul L. *Longing for Enough in a Culture of More.* Nashville, Abingdon Press, 2007.

Fletcher, Colin. *River: One Man's Journey Down the Colorado, Source to Sea.* New York: Alfred A. Knopf, 1997.

Flexner, James Thomas. *George Washington: Anguish and Farewell (1793-1799).* Boston: Little, Brown, and Company, 1972.

Gandhi, Mahatma. *All Men Are Brothers: Autobiographic Reflections.* New York, Continuum Publishing, 1997.

Gilbert, Sir Martin. *Churchill: A Life.* New York: Henry Holt and Company, 1991.

------ *In Search of Churchill: A Historian's Journey.* New York: John Wiley and Sons, 1994.

------ *Winston Churchill: The Wilderness Years.* Boston: Houghton Mifflin Company, 1982.

Goodwin, Doris Kearns. *Team of Rivals: The Political Genius of Abraham Lincoln.* New York: Simon & Schuster, 2005.

Hackworth, David H., and Julie Sherman. *About Face: The Odyssey of an American Warrior.* New York: Touchstone, 1989.

Hackworth, David H., and Eilhys England. *Steel My Soldiers' Hearts.* New York: Touchstone, 2003.

Harris, Burton. *John Colter: His Years in the Rockies.* Lincoln, NE: University of Nebraska Press, 1993.

Harris, David. *The Last Stand: The War Between Wall Street and Main Street over California's Ancient Redwoods.* San Francisco: Sierra Club, 1996.

Halberstam, David. *Firehouse.* New York: Buena Vista Books, 2002.

Hickman, Tom. *Churchill's Bodyguard: The Authorized Biography of Walter H. Thompson.* London: Headline Book Publishing, 2005.

Higgins, Marguerite. *Our Vietnam Nightmare.* New York: Harper & Row Publishers, 1965.

Hornfischer, James D. *The Last Stand of the Tin Can Sailors.* New York: Bantam Books, 2004.

James, D. Clayton. *The Years of MacArthur: Volume I 1880-1941.* Boston: Houghton Mifflin Company, 1970.

------ *The Years of MacArthur: Volume 2 1941-1945.* Boston: Houghton Mifflin Company, 1975.

------ *The Years of MacArthur Volume 3 Triumph and Disaster 1945-1964* Boston: Houghton Mifflin Company, 1985.

Jamison, Kay Redfield. *Exuberance: the Passion for Life.* New York: Alfred A. Knopf, 2004.

Jappy, M. J. *Danger UXB: The Remarkable Story of the Disposal of Unexploded Bombs during the Second World Was.* London: Pan Macmillian, 2001.

Johnson, Paul. *Heroes: From Alexander the Great and Julius Caesar to Churchill and De Gaulle.* New York: HarperCollins Publishers, 2007.

Kennedy, John F. *Profiles in Courage.* New York, HarperCollins Publishers, 1955.

Klein, Allen. *The Courage to Laug: Humor, Hope, and Healing in the Face of Death and Dying.* New York: Penguin Putnam, 1998.

Knight, Ian. *Rorke's Drift 1879.* Westport, CT: Praeger Publishers, 2005

Knight, Roger: *The Pursuit of Victory: The Life and Achievement of Horatio Nelson.* New York: Basic Books, 2005.

Korda, Michael. *Ike: An American Hero.* New York: HarperCollins Publishers, 2007.

Krakauer, Jon. *Into Thin Air.* New York: Villard Books, 1997.

Kryske, Larry. *The Churchill Factors: Creating Your Finest Hour.* Victoria, British Columbia: Trafford Publishing, 2000.

------ *The Greatest Board in the World.* Victoria, British Columbia: Trafford Publishing, 2003.

Kryske, Naomi. *The Witness (manuscript)*. Plano, TX: 2008.

L'Amour, Louis. *Education of a Wondering Man*. New York: Bantam, 1989.

Langguth, A. J. *Patriots: The Men Who Started the American Revolution*. New York: Simon & Schuster, 1988.

Lawrence, Thomas Edward. *Seven Pillars of Wisdom*. Garden City: NY: Double, Doran & Company, 1935.

Lukacs, John. *Five Days in London: May 1940*. New Haven: Yale University Press, 1999.

MacArthur, Douglas. *Reminiscences*. New York: McGraw Hill, 1964.

Manchester, William. *American Caesar: Douglas MacArthur 1880-1964*. Boston: Little, Brown, and Company, 1978.

------ *Goodbye, Darkness: A Memoir of the Pacific War*. New York: Dell, 1987.

------ *The Last Lion Winston Spencer Churchill: Visions of Glory 1874-1932*. Boston, Little, Brown and Company, 1983.

------ *The Last Lion Winston Spencer Churchill: Alone 1932-1040*. Boston: Little, Brown and Company, 1988.

McCain, John and Mark Salter. *Why Courage Matters: The Way to a Braver Life*. New York: Random House, 2004.

McCullough, David. *Brave Companions: Portraits in History*. New York: Simon and Schuster, 1992.

------ *The Path Between the Seas: The Creation of the Panama Canal 1870-1914*. New York: Simon and Schuster, 1977.

------ *Truman*. New York: Simon & Schuster, 1992.

Middlebrook, Martin. First Day on the Somme. New York: W. W. Norton and Company, 1972.

Miller, William Ian. *The Mystery of Courage*. Cambridge, MA: Harvard University Press, 2000.

Moore, Harold G., and Joseph L. Galloway. *We were Soldiers Once ... And Young: Ia Drang—the Battle that Changed the War in Vietnam*. New York: HarperTorch, 1992.

Moore, Patrick. *80 Not Out: The Autobiography*. London: Contender Books, 2003.

Moran, Lord. *The Anatomy of Courage*. Garden City, NY: Avery Publishing Group, 1987.

Patton, George S., Jr. *War As I Knew It*. Boston: Houghton Mifflin Company, 1947.

Perrett, Bryan. *Last Stand: Famous Battles Against the Odds*. Edison, NJ: Castle Books, 1998.

Persico, Joseph E. *Eleventh Month, Eleventh Day, Eleventh Hour: Armistice Day, 1918, World War I and Its Violent Climax*. New York: Random House, 2004.

Plumb, Joseph Charles. *I'm No Hero*. Independence, MO: Independence Press. 1973.

Polmar, Norman and Thomas B. Allen. *Rickover: Controversy and Genius.* New York: Simon and Schuster, 1982.

Potter, E.B. *Admiral Arleigh Burke: A Biography*. New York: Random House, 1990.

Powell, John Wesley. *The Exploration of the Colorado River and Its Canyons*. New York: Dover Publications, 1961.

Prochnau, William. *Once Upon a Distant War: Reporting from Vietnam*. Edinburgh: Mainstream Publishing. 1996.

Reisner, Marc. *Cadillac Desert: The American West and Its Disappearing Water*. New York: Viking Penguin, 1986.

Roberts, Randy, and James E. Olson. *A Line in the Sand: The Alamo in Blood and Memory*. New York: The Free Press, 2001.

Rowe, James N. *Five Years to Freedom*. New York: Ballantine Books, 1971.

Russell, Douglas S. *Winston Churchill Soldier: The Military Life of a Gentleman at War*. London: Brassey's, 2005

Salisbury, Gay and Laney Salisbury. *The Cruelest Miles: The Heroic Story of Dogs and Men in a Race Against an Epidemic*. New York: W.W. Norton and Company, 2003.

Sandys, Celia. *Churchill Wanted Dead or Alive.* New York: Carroll & Graf Publishers, 1999.

Sassoon, Siegfried. *Memoirs of an Infantry Officer.* London: Faber and Faber, 1965.

Strickland, Matthew and Robert Hardy. *The Great Warbow: From Hastings to the Mary Rose.* Phoenix Mill, UK: Sutton Publishing, 2005.

Stockdale, James Bond and Sybil Stockdale. *In Love and War: The Story of a Family's Ordeal and Sacrifice during the Vietnam Years.* New York: HarperCollins Publishers, 1984.

Stone, Irving. *Depths of Glory: A Biographical Novel of Camille Pissarro.* New York: Doubleday & Company, 1985.

Thatcher, Margaret. *The Downing Street Years.* New York: HarperCollins Publishers, 1993.

Trulock, Alice Rains. *In the Hands of Providence: Joshua Lawrence Chamberlain and the American Civil War.* Chapel Hill, NC: University of North Carolina Press, 1992.

United States Naval Institute. *Watch Officer's Guide: A Handbook for All Deck Watch Officers, 10th Edition.* Annapolis, MD: Naval Institute Press, 1971.

Warden, Herbert W. III (editor). *American Courage: Remarkable True Stories Exhibiting Bravery that has Made Our Country Great.* New York: HarperCollins Publishers, 2005.

Warren, Stephen G. *Flying into Combat with Heroes.* Baltimore: Publish America, 2003.

White, W. L. *They Were Expendable.* New York: Harcourt, Brace and Company, 1942.

Winters, Dick. *Beyond the Band of Brothers: The War Memoirs of Major Dick Winters.* New York: Berkley Publishing, 2006.

Worster, Donald. *A River Running West: The Life of John Wesley Powell.* Oxford: Oxford University Press, 2001.

Also by Lawrence M. Kryske

The Chuᴝchill Factors: Creating Your Finest Hour

Brings new insights about leadership. This readable book can be called "applied Churchill." The Reporter's Approach™ provides a powerful methodology for strategic planning and goal setting that succeeds where other systems have failed. Using the Churchill Factors—Churchill's best practices involving leadership—readers will learn how they can achieve heroic results, harness relentless resolve, and turn adversity into advantage. Rev. 2002, 232 pages, 6" x 9" trade paperback, $20.

The Greatest Board in the World

Written in parable format. Describes how a trade association's board of directors was able to become an extraordinary team and create a winning association. Provides proven leadership and teamwork tips to help teams work together better, anticipate and minimize misunderstandings and conflicts, build more effective communications strategies, and how to value the differences among team members. Rev. 2004, 113 pages, 6" x 9" trade paperback, $13.

About the Author

Commander Lawrence M. (Larry) Kryske, U.S. Navy (Ret.) develops victorious leaders who have vision, courage, and determination. He is a professional speaker, certified trainer, facilitator, and coach who has over thirty-five years of worldwide success leading men and women and building unstoppable teams. He has been a career naval officer and private school administrator.

With Admiral James Stockdale   With General Colin Powell

Larry is president of Your Finest Hour Leadership Programs, a full-service leadership development business that started in 1996. He speaks nationwide on leadership, teamwork, and productivity. He has given keynotes, conducted training seminars, and facilitated leadership retreats for over 400 corporate, nonprofit (trade associations), governmental, educational, and civic organizations in 50 different industries.

Larry is a respected authority on the life and leadership of Winston Churchill with over 40 years of Churchill study. He is also the author of the leadership books, *The Churchill Factors: Creating Your Finest Hour* and *The Greatest Board in the World*.

Larry has a BA in Astronomy from the University of California at Los Angeles (UCLA) and a MS in Applied Science from the Naval Postgraduate School in Monterey, CA. He resides in Plano, Texas, a northern suburb of Dallas.

Contact the author at:

Larry@YourFinestHour.com   www.YourFinestHour.com

CPSIA information can be obtained at www.ICGtesting.com
Printed in the USA
241200LV00007B/4/P